Monster Creatures of the Deep Sea

2nd Edition

by David E. McAdams

http://www.demcadams.com

Illustration 1: Cold deep corals in the Bay of Biscay

Copyright 2025, David E. McAdams. All rights reserved. No part of this book may be reproduced by any means, in any form, or be digitally recorded or transmitted in any manner without express written consent of the author.

Many images in this book are licensed. No licensed image may be reproduced by any means without permission of the copyright holder. For more information, see image credits, page 98.

Other Books by David E. McAdams

Colors: **Parrot Colors**, **Flower Colors**, **Space Colors**, **People Colors**, **Royal Colors** – Introduces the concept of colors using beautiful themed images, ages 0-6.

Learning Numbers: **The Dragon Number Book**, **The Elvish Number Book**, **The Fairy Number Book**, **Red Neck Number Book**, **The Unicorn Number Book**, **The Truck Number Book**, **Anna's Seasons** – Enjoy learning the numbers 0-10 with fabulous themed images, ages 2-7.

Number Coloring Books: **Number Coloring Book**, **Dragon Numbers Coloring Book**, **Animal Numbers Coloring Book, Muscle Car Number Coloring Book** and **Geometric Shapes Coloring Book** – Provide hours of fun while teaching number recognition, ages 3-8.

Arithmetic:

Numbers – A beginner-friendly book introducing the concept of numbers. Recommended for ages 5-7.

One Penny, Two – Join Jerry on his journey to buy a sports car as his penny doubles each day. For ages 8-12.

Rhyme and Reason – A fun set of 229 math puzzles, ages 6-7 years old.

Amazing Numbers – Worksheets with mazes to reinforce sequence, count by's and other early learner math skills.

One and One – Join these friends as they learn addition from colorful, fun scenarios.

Safari Times – Safari Times is a thrilling expedition into the world of multiplication, where math meets the wild!

Fraction Feast – Fraction Feast uses illustrated foods to introduce children to the world of fractions in a way that's fun.

Learning With Play Money Activity Kit – A fun hands-on kit to teach counting and large numbers. Best for ages 8-12.

Geometry:

Shapes, **Shapes Two**, **Shapes 3-D** – A playful introduction to geometric shapes, ages 3-8.

Geometric Nets Project Book (80 nets), **Geometric Nets Mega Project Book** (253 geometric nets) – Features geometric nets to copy, cut out, and construct into 3D polyhedra, ages 9 and up.

Theory and Reference:

What is Bigger Than Anything? (Infinity) – A fascinating look at the concept of infinity for curious minds aged 6-8.

Swing Sets (Set Theory) – A comprehensive introduction to set theory, tailored for students aged 7-10.

Time is Totally Weird – A tweens guide to one of the most bizarre things in physics: time!

All Math Words Dictionary – A comprehensive math dictionary covering key concepts in pre-algebra, algebra, geometry, and pre-calculus.

Life lessons:

If I Had a Monster – A charming story where monsters represent important people in a child's life. Fun for all ages.

Growing Up and Up and Up – A heartwarming voyage sharing joy in life's stages.

Even Generals Take Out the Garbage – A heartwarming story that teaches children the importance of doing chores. Suitable for young readers.

Think Like a Genius! – An inspirational review of mathematicians and scientists through the ages with lessons drawn from each life.

Hogwash! Living a Baloney Free Life – how to notice and reject nonsense.

Mind benders: **50 Riddles**, **Mazes Galore**, **My Favorite Fractals (Volumes 1 & 2)** – A visual treat of high-resolution fractal images, appealing to all ages.

For the Math Enthusiast: **The First Million Digits of Pi**, **The First Million Digits of e**, **The Square Root of 2 to One Million Digits**, **The First Hundred Thousand Prime Numbers** – Impress your family and friends with these handy references featuring important math constants, suitable for all ages.

For more information and an up-to-date list of books, visit https://www.DEMcAdams.com.

Table of Contents

Preface 1
Life 1
Life on Land 3
Life in the Ocean 3
Geography of the Ocean 4
Nutrients in the Ocean 5
Zones of the Ocean 6
Oceans of the World 15
Carbon Cycle and the Ocean: Nature's Exchange of Life and Element
.... 15
Phytoplankton: Microscopic Powerhouses of the Ocean 17
Zooplankton: Drifting Animals of the Ocean 18
Parts of a Fish: Form and Function Beneath the Waves 20
New Wonders of the Deep (2023–2025) 21
Atlantic Hagfish: Slimemaster 24
Barreleye: The See-Through Spectacle 25
Black Swallower: Eats Fish Larger Than Itself 26
Blobfish: A Gelatinous Mass 28
Bluefin Tuna: A Warm Blooded Fish 29
Blue Goo: What Are You? 30
Bluntnose Sixgill Shark: Sibling Rivalry to the Max 31
Chambered Nautilus: A Spit Machine 33
Coelacanth: Master of Chill 35
Cookiecutter Shark: The Bite-Sized Terror 36
Cuvier's Beaked Whale: The Deep Diving Champion! 38
Deep Sea Anglerfish: A Light in the Dark 39
Deep Sea Coral: Nature's Deep Sea Art 40
Deep Sea Dragonfish: Terrors of the Deep 42
Dumbo Octopus: Flappy Eared Wonder 43
Fangtooth: Tiny Terror with a Giant Bite 45
Firefly Squid: Light Show In the Sea 46
Flabby Whalefish: Transformers of the Sea 48
Frilled Shark: A Fossil With Fangs 49
Giant Isopod: Giant Deep-Sea Rolly-Polly 50
Giant Tube Worms: The Mouthless Marvels 52
Goblin Shark: Fish With an Electric Nose 54

Gummy Squirrel: Sea Cucumber That Looks Like Candy..................55
Helmet Jellyfish: Glowing Red Helmet...56
Japanese Spider Crab: The Gentle Giant with Sticky Style..................58
Lanternfish: Tiny Swimmers, Big Light Show..59
Long Nosed Chimaera: Jet-Nosed Ghost of the Deep..........................60
Mariana Snailfish: Champion of the Abyss...61
Marine Hatchetfish: Shadow Snatcher..62
Megamouth Shark: Eats Like a Whale..64
Oarfish: Sea Serpent of the Deep...65
Pompeii worm: The Hottest Home on Earth..67
Sea Angel: Winged Wonder...68
Sea Pig: Party Animal of the Deep..69
Sea Toad: Lure-Master of the Deep..70
Siphonophore: The Colony That Pretends to Be One Animal..............72
Slender Snipe Eel: Duck Beak on a String...74
Sperm Whale: Deep Diving Mammal..75
Tripod Fish: Out of the Mud...76
Tube Worms: Methane Munchers of the Deep.....................................78
Umbrella Mouth Gulper Eel: Huge Mouth...79
Vampire Squid: With a Cloak and Eyes That Glow...............................80
Viperfish: Fish With Fangs..82
Zombie Worm: Bone-Eaters of the Deep..83
Learning Activities...85
   Predator/Prey Activity: A Game of Vibrations and Stealth..............85
   Water Pressure Activity: Deep Dive..86
   Density Activity: Sink or Float?..87
   Water Temperature And Density Activity..88
Glossary...91
IPA Pronunciation...97
Image Credits..98

Preface

In recent years, scientists have ventured into the deepest parts of our planet's oceans. Many expected to find vast, lifeless expanses. Instead, what they discovered was astonishing, a hidden world teeming with strange and remarkable life forms.

Far beneath the ocean's surface dwell creatures that challenge the imagination. In this dark, cold, and high-pressure environment, life has evolved in extraordinary ways. With minimal oxygen, scarce food, and a complete absence of sunlight, these deep-sea organisms have developed a remarkable range of adaptations. Some possess enormous jaws, others produce their own light, and many appear like monsters from a science fiction story.

In this book, you will encounter the bizarre and the breathtaking:
- How does a creature without a mouth consume its food? Discover the mystery of zombie worms and giant tube worms.
- Why does the blobfish resemble a jelly-like mass rather than a typical fish?
- What deep-sea predator carves two-inch circles of flesh from its prey using razor-like teeth?
- Which fish can swallow prey ten times its size, but risks death if it miscalculates?
- What animals have changed little since the time of the dinosaurs?
- Which fish begins digestion while still inside its prey?
- Why do some deep-sea creatures generate their own light in complete darkness?
- Why do so many deep-ocean fish have disproportionately large mouths?
- Which shark prefers plankton over meat?
- What creature moves by forcefully expelling water from its body?
- Which predator specializes in pulling snails out of their shells before devouring them?

These are just a few of the fascinating questions explored in *Monster Creatures of the Deep Sea*. Prepare to meet the ocean's most astonishing and otherworldly inhabitants, living proof that even in the harshest environments, life finds a way.

Life

Life can be found in nearly every environment on Earth: in the air, on the land, beneath the soil, and throughout the oceans. Regardless of where it exists, all life requires three essential components: a source of energy, a method to transform that energy into the living matter that makes up its body, and a way to reproduce.

Most of the energy for life forms on our planet comes from the sun. Through a process called photosynthesis, plants capture sunlight and use it to convert water, carbon dioxide, and minerals into the building blocks of plant tissue. Animals then eat these plants, using the stored energy to build and maintain their own bodies. In digesting this material, animals consume oxygen and release carbon dioxide back into the environment. Some of the plant matter becomes part of the animal's body, while the rest is excreted as feces (waste).

Many animals, known as predators, obtain energy by eating other animals, called prey. In doing so, they absorb the nutrients and the energy stored in their prey. Over time, all living things, both plants and animals, die. Their remains are broken down by decomposers such as bacteria, fungi, and insects. These organisms return vital elements to the environment in a continuous process known as the carbon cycle[1].

However, not all life depends on the sun. Certain bacteria thrive deep within the Earth or at the bottom of the ocean, where sunlight cannot reach. These bacteria obtain energy from chemicals released by sources such as underwater volcanic vents. In these ecosystems, bacteria form the base of the food chain. Other organisms feed on the bacteria, and predators feed on those organisms, sustaining a unique community of life far removed from sunlight.

Reproduction, the process by which life creates new life, also varies widely. Most methods fall into two primary categories: sexual and asexual reproduction. In sexual reproduction, offspring are formed when an egg cell from the mother, containing half the genetic material, combines with a sperm cell from the father, which contains the other half. In asexual reproduction, a single organism produces offspring without a partner, often by dividing or budding, resulting in a new individual with identical or nearly identical DNA.

In the mysterious depths of the ocean, where sunlight fades and pressure rises, life continues to flourish in extraordinary ways. This book explores the strange and often monstrous creatures that inhabit these deep-sea realms, revealing the powerful forces of evolution and adaptation at work beneath the waves.

---

[1] See Carbon Cycle and the Ocean on page 15.

Life on Land

Nearly all life on land exists within a few hundred feet of the Earth's surface. Even birds, though capable of flight, must eventually return to the ground to rest. This limitation is due to a basic property of matter: density.

Density is the amount of mass contained in a specific volume[2]. To understand this concept, imagine three identical drinking glasses. Leave one empty (it will contain only air), fill the second with water, and the third with sand. Though the glasses are the same size, they feel different in weight. The glass filled with sand will feel heaviest because sand is denser than water or air. The more mass a substance contains in a given volume, the greater its density.

Living organisms, whether plants or animals, are largely composed of water and organic molecules. Water, in its liquid form, is much denser than air. When water vapor condenses into droplets, it becomes too dense to remain suspended in the atmosphere and falls to the ground as rain or snow. Because of this, most life that relies on air is naturally limited to the layers of the atmosphere and land closest to the Earth's surface.

In contrast, life in the ocean is not limited in the same way. The ocean, being a dense fluid itself, provides support for life at a vast range of depths. Unlike air, water can carry organisms far below the surface. down into regions where light fades, pressure rises, and temperatures fall. These conditions, while extreme, are not empty or lifeless. Instead, they are home to some of the most unusual and fascinating creatures on the planet.

In the deep ocean, life has evolved to thrive in environments far removed from the surface. In this book, *Monster Creatures of the Deep Sea*, we will explore these mysterious regions and meet the extraordinary organisms that call the depths their home.

Life in the Ocean

Because the ocean is composed of water, and most living organisms are also largely made of water, the density of marine plants and animals is very similar to that of the surrounding seawater. As a result, many ocean creatures do not need to find a solid surface to rest upon. Instead, they are able to float or swim continuously throughout their lives. This unique quality of the marine environment allows life to exist at every depth, from the sunlit surface waters to the darkest and deepest ocean trenches.

However, as one travels deeper into the ocean, several environmental conditions change dramatically:
- The amount of light decreases until complete darkness prevails.
- The density of the water increases.

---

[2] See *Density Activity*, page 87.

- Water pressure rises a lot.
- Oxygen becomes less available.

These changing factors influence what kinds of organisms can survive at various depths and what special adaptations are necessary for life in each zone. To better understand and describe the conditions found at different depths, scientists have divided the ocean into several distinct regions, known as ocean zones.

The chapter titled *Zones of the Ocean* explores each of these regions, providing an introduction to the environmental challenges found there and the remarkable creatures that have adapted to thrive in them.

Geography of the Ocean

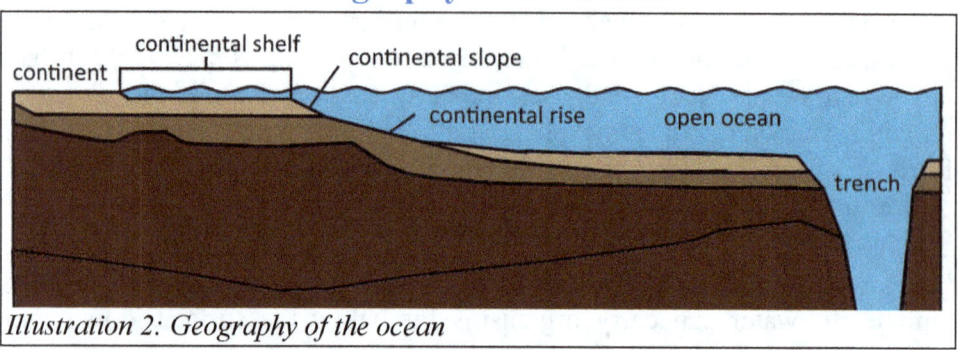

Illustration 2: Geography of the ocean

The ocean is divided into several distinct regions, each with unique characteristics that influence the types of life forms that can survive there. One of the most important of these regions is the continental shelf: a relatively shallow area that extends outward from the edge of a continent. This shelf is composed of sediment, soil, and organic material carried by rivers and streams from the land. As a result, the continental shelf is rich in nutrients, making it a highly productive zone for marine life.

Beyond the continental shelf lies the continental slope, a much steeper area that descends rapidly into deeper waters. Although it also receives nutrients from land, the slope contains fewer resources than the shelf above it.

Further down is the continental rise, located between the continental slope and the deep ocean floor. This zone is formed by sediment that accumulates as it slides down the slope. The steepness of the rise helps channel falling organic material, often called marine snow, toward the deep ocean.

Beneath all these zones lies the abyssal plain, a vast, mostly flat region that forms much of the ocean floor. Marine snow, made up of tiny particles of dead organisms and organic matter, settles here and becomes the primary source of energy for many deep-sea creatures.

In some areas of the abyssal plain, there are trenches: narrow, extremely deep valleys with steep sides. These geological features are created where tectonic plates meet and one plate is forced beneath another. Life does exist in these trenches, but it is often sparsely distributed, as food is harder to find.

The ocean floor also hosts volcanoes and hydrothermal vents, including features known as black smokers. Some undersea volcanoes eventually grow tall enough to become islands. These geological formations are not only important in shaping the structure of the seafloor but also provide mineral-rich chemicals that support odd ecosystems, often independent of sunlight.

Illustration 3: Black smokers

Nutrients in the Ocean

All living organisms require certain things from the environment in order to survive and thrive. These essential resources include minerals, water, and sources of energy such as food. In the ocean, the availability and distribution of nutrients vary greatly depending on depth, location, and geological activity.

Marine plants, such as phytoplankton and algae, absorb nutrients like nitrates and phosphates directly from the water. Using sunlight through the process of photosynthesis, these plants convert these nutrients into energy and biomass. Animals in the ocean rely on these plants for nourishment, or consume other animals that have fed on plant matter.

In the deep sea, far below the reach of sunlight, nutrients are often supplied in different ways. One major source is marine snow. Marine snow is a continuous shower of organic particles that drifts down from the upper ocean layers. Another important source of nutrients is river runoff, which delivers minerals and organic materials into coastal regions and the open sea.

Remarkably, some deep-sea ecosystems are sustained by nutrients that do not originate from the sunlit surface at all. Underwater volcanoes and hydrothermal vents, including structures known as black smokers, release mineral-rich chemicals into the surrounding water. Specialized bacteria consume these chemicals through a process called chemosynthesis, forming the base of a unique food web that supports a variety of deep-sea organisms.

In certain areas of the Pacific Ocean, ocean currents prevent nutrients from rising to the surface, resulting in limited biological activity in the upper layers. Also, these same nutrients accumulate at the seafloor, supporting a surprising abundance of life in the depths.

Zones of the Ocean

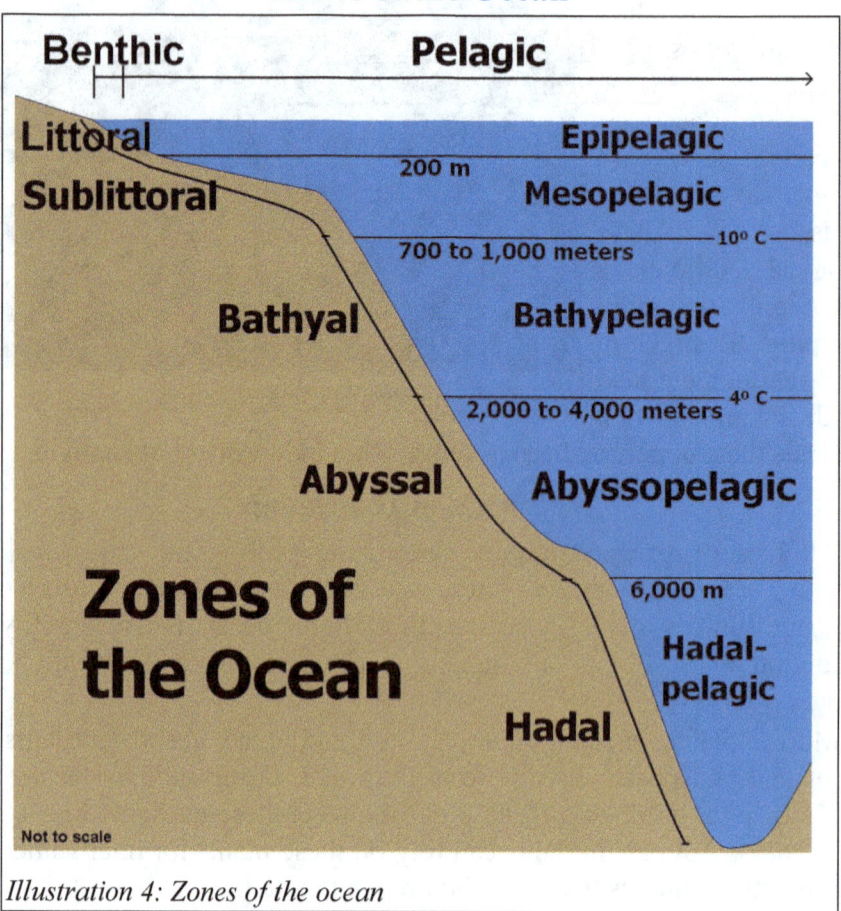

Illustration 4: Zones of the ocean

To better understand where marine organisms live, scientists have classified the ocean into two major zones based on their relationship to the coast or seafloor: the benthic zone and the pelagic zone.

Benthic Zone

The Benthic Zone refers to areas that are located on or very near the ocean floor, both in shallow water and deep water. Organisms that live in this zone, known as benthic organisms, may dwell along the shoreline, on the continental shelf, or even in the deepest ocean trenches. These creatures are adapted to living in close contact with the seabed, where they may burrow into sediment, cling to rocks, or crawl along the ocean floor.

Pelagic Zone

In contrast, the pelagic zone encompasses the vast open waters of the ocean that are neither near the seafloor nor the coastal boundaries. This zone is sometimes referred to as the "open ocean". Marine life found in this zone, called pelagic organisms, spend their lives swimming or drifting in the water column, far from the ocean bottom. These include animals such as jellyfish, tuna, and whales, which are specially adapted to life in the open sea.

Understanding the difference between these zones helps scientists classify marine life and study how different species interact with their environments.

Zones by Depth

Both the benthic (seafloor) and pelagic (open water) zones of the ocean are further divided into five depth-based zones, each defined by its distance from the surface and its temperature. These zones differ in several important ways that influence which species can survive there and how they adapt to the environment.

Four main environmental factors change with depth:
- The amount of sunlight and heat from the sun,
- The temperature of the water,
- The pressure[3] exerted by the weight of the water above, and
- The availability of oxygen in the water.

The sun plays a central role in shaping conditions at the ocean's surface. Sunlight provides both light and heat, warming the surface layers and driving the process of photosynthesis in ocean plants. Without the sun, Earth would be a frozen planet, and liquid water, which is the foundation of life as we know it, would not exist. Nearly all forms of life on Earth depend on water to grow, reproduce, and survive.

One unusual property of water makes life in the deep sea possible: the relationship between temperature and density. Most materials become denser as they get colder[4]. Water does too, until it reaches 4° Celsius (39° Fahrenheit). At this point, water reaches its maximum density. Colder water, such as ice at 0°C (32°F), is actually less dense and floats. If this were not the case, ice would sink, and the deep ocean would eventually freeze solid. Instead, cold, dense 4°C water settles at the ocean's bottom,

---

[3] See *Water Pressure* activity, page 86.
[4] See *Water Density and Temperature* activity, page 88.

which is why most of the deepest parts of the ocean remain at this stable temperature.

Light is another crucial factor that influences life in the ocean[5]. Plants near the surface use sunlight to convert water, air, and minerals into organic matter, a process that stores solar energy in plant tissues. These plants are consumed by herbivores (plant-eating animals), which in turn are eaten by carnivores (meat-eating animals). When these creatures die, their energy is recycled by scavengers, fungi, and bacteria, which eat their remains.

Sunlight, however, does not reach the entire ocean. As light passes through water, each layer absorbs some of it, allowing less and less to pass through. The topmost part of the ocean, down to about 200 meters (approximately 650 feet), is called the photic zone, meaning "lighted zone." This is where most photosynthesis occurs. Below this depth lies the aphotic zone, meaning "without light." While it is not completely dark and some faint light may penetrate, there is so little light that it becomes extremely dim, and photosynthesis can no longer take place.

These variations in light, heat, pressure, and oxygen across ocean layers create a complex environment where only specially adapted organisms can survive at each depth.

The Epipelagic Zone: Sunlit Surface Waters

The epipelagic zone is the top layer of the ocean, going from the surface to a depth of approximately 200 meters (about 650 feet). This zone is often referred to as the sunlight zone because it receives enough sunlight to support photosynthesis, the process by which plants and some microorganisms convert light energy into food.

Illustration 5: Kelp forest

In this zone, marine algae, particularly microscopic, single-celled organisms known as phytoplankton, play a crucial role. Although they lack roots, stems, and leaves like land plants, phytoplankton harness sunlight to grow and

---

5 See *Light Absorption* activity, page 89.

reproduce. Rather than producing seeds, these tiny plants multiply by cell division, where one cell splits into two. Each new cell continues to absorb sunlight and convert it into energy, forming the base of the marine food web.

Seaweed and other plant-like organisms also thrive in this zone, especially near coastal areas where they can anchor themselves. In the open ocean, however, phytoplankton are the primary producers and form the foundation of life.

Many small marine animals feed directly on these microscopic plants. These herbivores (plant eaters) are in turn eaten by larger predators. In this way, solar energy is passed through the food chain, from algae to herbivores to carnivores, supporting a wide variety of marine life.

The temperature of the epipelagic zone varies greatly depending on geographic location. Near the poles, the water is close to freezing, while in tropical regions, it can reach temperatures similar to that of the human body. These temperature differences are caused by the varying intensity of sunlight at different latitudes (different distances from the equator).

The epipelagic zone contains the highest concentration of life in the ocean, including many species of bacteria, plankton, fish, and marine mammals. Because sunlight cannot penetrate beyond this layer, photosynthesis cannot occur in deeper zones, making the epipelagic zone a critical source of energy for organisms that live far below. Nutrients and organic material produced here often sink and become the primary food supply for many deep-sea ecosystems.

Mesopelagic Zone: The Twilight Depths

Illustration 6: Sabertooth fish from the mesopelagic zone

The mesopelagic zone, often referred to as the "twilight zone," lies beneath the sunlit surface waters of the ocean. The term "twilight" describes the time of day just after sunset, when light still lingers but darkness begins to take hold. Similarly, this oceanic zone receives only faint, filtered sunlight. This level of light is insufficient to support most photosynthetic plant life.

At the same depth along the seafloor lies a portion of the benthic zone known as the sublittoral zone. This area, though still part of the continental shelf, receives little light and harbors a distinct range of organisms adapted to dim environments.

Temperatures in the mesopelagic zone vary significantly, ranging from values close to the ocean's surface temperature down to approximately 10°C (50°F). This transition in temperature occurs within a layer known as the thermocline, where the water cools rapidly the deeper it goes.

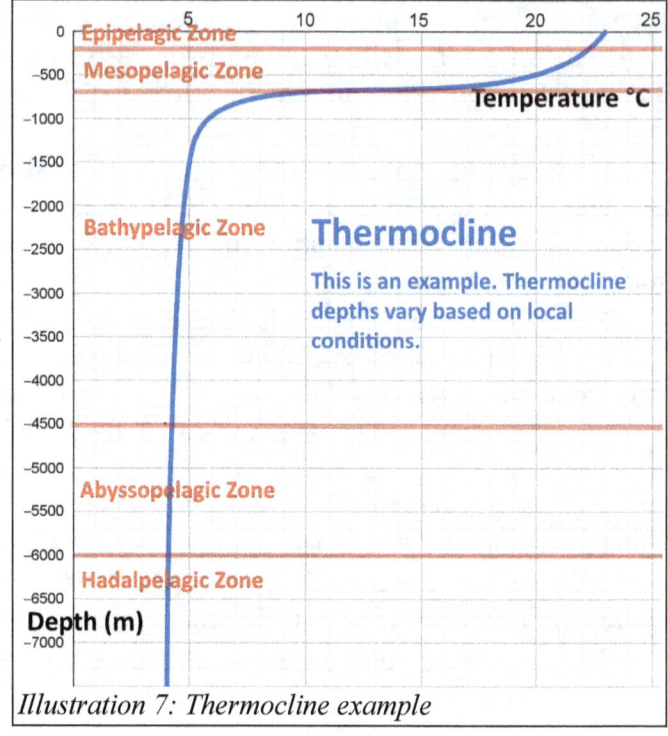

Illustration 7: Thermocline example

Many creatures that inhabit the mesopelagic zone engage in a daily vertical migration. During the day, they remain in the relative safety of the twilight zone, avoiding predators that rely on sight. At night, they ascend to the surface to feed, cloaked in darkness.

Food in this zone is limited, so many organisms rely on a things known as marine snow. Marine snow is a continuous shower of organic material falling from the upper layers of the ocean. Marine snow consists of the remains of dead or dying plants and animals, fecal matter, and other debris originating in the epipelagic (sunlit) zone above.

To survive in this dim environment, many mesopelagic species have developed special adaptations. Some produce their own light through a chemical process called bioluminescence, similar to that seen in fireflies. This light may serve various purposes: avoiding predators, luring prey, or communicating with other members of their species. Others have evolved unusually large eyes to gather as much light as possible from their surroundings.

Notable inhabitants of the mesopelagic zone include swordfish, various species of squid, and the predatory sabertooth fish, all uniquely suited to life in the twilight depths.

Bathypelagic Zone: The Deep Midnight

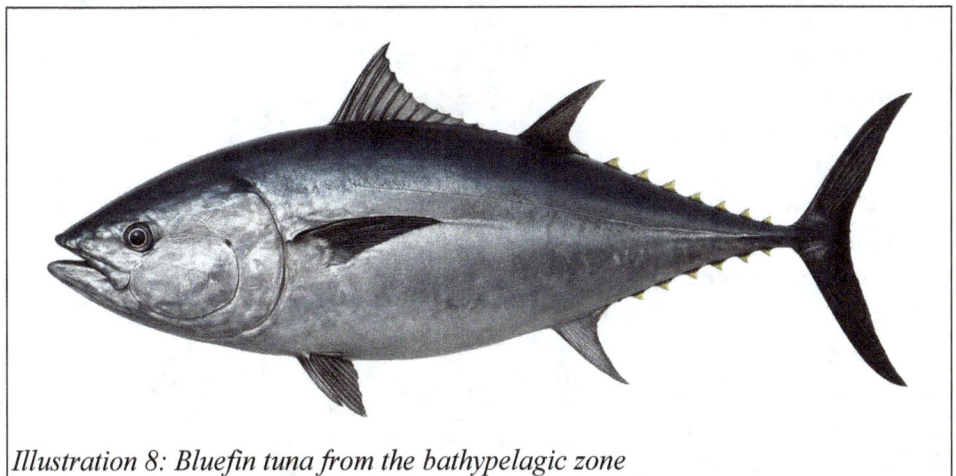
Illustration 8: Bluefin tuna from the bathypelagic zone

The bathypelagic zone marks the upper region of what scientists refer to as the midnight zone. It is a vast expanse of ocean where it is completely dark. Even on the clearest, starriest night, the sky above is far brighter than the water in this zone. The darkness here is nearly absolute, comparable to being inside a sealed, windowless closet on a cloudy night, with no trace of light slipping through.

Temperatures in the bathypelagic zone fall steadily with depth, ranging from about 10°C (50°F) near its upper boundary to approximately 4°C (39°F) at its deepest extent. The layer along the ocean floor at the same depth is known as the bathyal zone, part of the larger benthic zone, which refers to life near or on the ocean floor.

Due to the absence of sunlight, many organisms in the bathypelagic zone have evolved in remarkable ways. Some species lack eyes entirely, as sight offers no advantage in total darkness. Others produce their own light through bioluminescence, a biological process that allows them to glow in the dark. This light may be used to attract prey, communicate, and avoid predators.

Because food is extremely scarce at these depths, survival requires efficiency. Many animals in this zone have adapted by conserving energy. Instead of actively hunting, some drift slowly or remain motionless, conserving energy while waiting for food to pass by. As a result, these creatures often have small muscle mass, reflecting their low-energy lifestyle in one of the ocean's most extreme environments.

Abyssopelagic Zone: The Lightless Abyss

The abyssopelagic zone begins at the depth where seawater is fixed at approximately 4°C (39°F) and goes down to around 6,000 meters (20,000 feet) beneath the surface. This zone represents one of the deepest regions of the open ocean. Its counterpart along the seafloor is known as the abyssal zone or abyssal plane, part of the larger benthic zone, where life exists in contact with the ocean bottom.

The conditions in the abyssopelagic zone are extreme. Water pressure increases a lot with depth, reaching up to 76 megapascals, equivalent to about 11,000 pounds per square inch. This is more than 750 times the pressure found at sea level.

Illustration 9: Dumbo octopus from the abyssopelagic zone

Because sunlight does not reach these depths, plants cannot grow here. Most of the food available to organisms in this zone arrives from above, either as drifting organic material or as sediment washed down from higher levels of the ocean. This includes decomposing remains of marine life and other particulate matter that settles slowly through the water column.

To adapt to the scarcity of food, many animals in the abyssopelagic zone have evolved unique physical features. One common trait is a lower jaw that extends beyond the upper jaw, allowing these creatures to sift through the ocean floor in search of edible material hidden in the mud and sand.

Notable inhabitants of this zone include the black swallower, the tripod fish, the deep-sea anglerfish, and the elusive giant squid, all highly specialized for life in the cold, pressurized, and pitch-black waters of the deep ocean.

Hadalpelagic Zone: Life in the Ocean's Deepest Trenches

The hadalpelagic zone represents the deepest region of the ocean, found only within the world's deepest trenches. This zone begins at a depth of 6,000 meters (approximately 20,000 feet) and extends downward into the most deepest parts of the sea. The portion of the seafloor within this zone is referred to as the hadal zone, or the trench zone.

Illustration 10: Mariana snailfish in the hadalpelagic zone

For much of scientific history, scientists believed that no life could survive under the immense pressure and darkness of the hadalpelagic zone. However, modern deep-sea exploration has revealed that life does indeed exist in these extreme environments. Scientists have discovered a number of specialized organisms that thrive in the cold, dark, and high-pressure conditions of ocean trenches.

The primary sources of food in the hadal zone include marine snow, sinking animal carcasses, and nutrients released by hydrothermal vents.

- Marine snow consists of microscopic remains of dead plants and animals, as well as animal waste, drifting down from higher layers of the ocean.
- Bodies of larger dead animals, such as whales or fish, occasionally fall into trenches, providing temporary feasts for scavengers.
- Hydrothermal vents are cracks on the seafloor where water heated by magma (molten rock), rich in chemicals, escapes from beneath the Earth's crust. Bacteria near these vents use the chemicals in a process called chemosynthesis to produce energy, forming the foundation of an unusual deep-sea food chain. Other organisms, such as giant tube worms, feed on these bacteria or form symbiotic relationships with them. A symbiotic relationship is where both creatures help each other.

Despite the extreme conditions, several remarkable animals have been found in the hadalpelagic zone. These include deep-sea jellyfish, viperfish with their long, fang-like teeth, giant tube worms near hydrothermal vents, and slow-moving sea cucumbers, such as the gummy squirrel, that scavenge the ocean floor.

The existence of life in this hidden realm continues to challenge our understanding of biology and the limits of survival on Earth.

Thermal Vents: Life Without Sunlight

Illustration 11: Life at a thermal vent

Although thermal vents are not classified as one of the ocean's depth zones, they play a vital role in supporting unique ecosystems deep beneath the sea. A thermal vent, also known as a hydrothermal vent, is a place on the ocean floor where seawater comes into contact with magma, or molten rock, from beneath the Earth's crust.

These vents are usually found along mid-ocean ridges, where tectonic plates are moving apart and magma rises close to the seabed. Cold seawater seeps down into cracks in the ocean floor and encounters this magma. The water is superheated and infused with minerals and chemicals such as hydrogen sulfide. The heated water then rises back up through the seafloor, emerging from the vent in a stream that can reach temperatures of over 350°C (662°F). Despite the intense heat and pressure, life flourishes around these vents.

Unlike most life on Earth, which depends on sunlight for energy through the process of photosynthesis, the organisms living near thermal vents rely on a completely different energy source: chemosynthesis. At the base of these ecosystems are specialized chemosynthetic bacteria that eat the chemicals dissolved in the vent water, especially hydrogen sulfide, to produce energy and organic compounds. These bacteria serve the same role in the food chain that plants do in sunlit environments.

Various animals have adapted to this unusual environment by forming close relationships with these bacteria. Some, like giant tube worms, have no mouths or digestive systems at all; instead, they host bacteria inside their bodies consume the chemicals and provide the worms with nutrients. Other animals, such as vent crabs, blind shrimp, and vent mussels, eat the bacteria or feed on other creatures that rely on them.

The discovery of hydrothermal vent ecosystems has revolutionized our understanding of life's possibilities. It shows that life can thrive in complete darkness, under immense pressure, and without sunlight, raising exciting questions about the potential for life in similar extreme environments on other planets or moons.

Oceans of the World

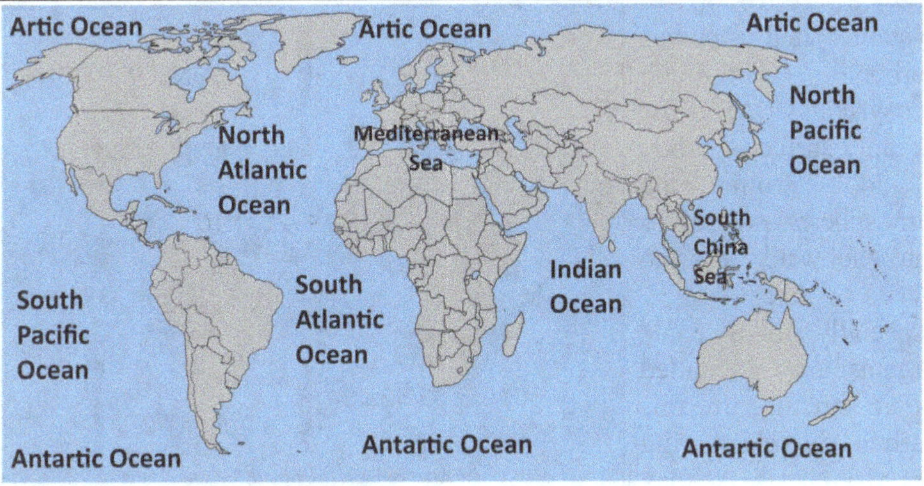

Illustration 12: Oceans of the world

Carbon Cycle and the Ocean: Nature's Exchange of Life and Element

Carbon is a fundamental building block of life. Carbon is present in every living organism on Earth. Through the natural process of photosynthesis, plants absorb carbon dioxide (CO_2) and water from their environment to produce energy-rich compounds. These compounds form the tissues (leaves, stems, and roots) that support plant life. In this process, carbon atoms from the air are transformed into the substance of living things.

When herbivores eat plants, they absorb carbon into their own bodies. Carnivores, which feed on herbivores and other carnivores, continue the flow of carbon through the food chain. At each stage, carbon becomes a part of muscles, bones and other tissues.

When a plant or animal dies, decomposers such as bacteria, fungi, and scavengers break down the remains. In doing so, they release some carbon back into the air as carbon dioxide and store some in the soil and sediment. Part of this carbon may stay buried for centuries or even millions of years, forming part of the Earth's long-term carbon storage. This continuous exchange of carbon between the atmosphere, organisms, soil, and the ocean is known as the carbon cycle.

The ocean plays an important role in the carbon cycle. It acts as both a sink (a place where carbon is stored) and a conveyor (a system that moves carbon through ecosystems). At the ocean's surface, carbon dioxide from the atmosphere dissolves into the water. Marine plants and algae, especially microscopic organisms called phytoplankton, use this carbon dioxide during photosynthesis. As they grow, they store carbon in their tissues and release oxygen into the water.

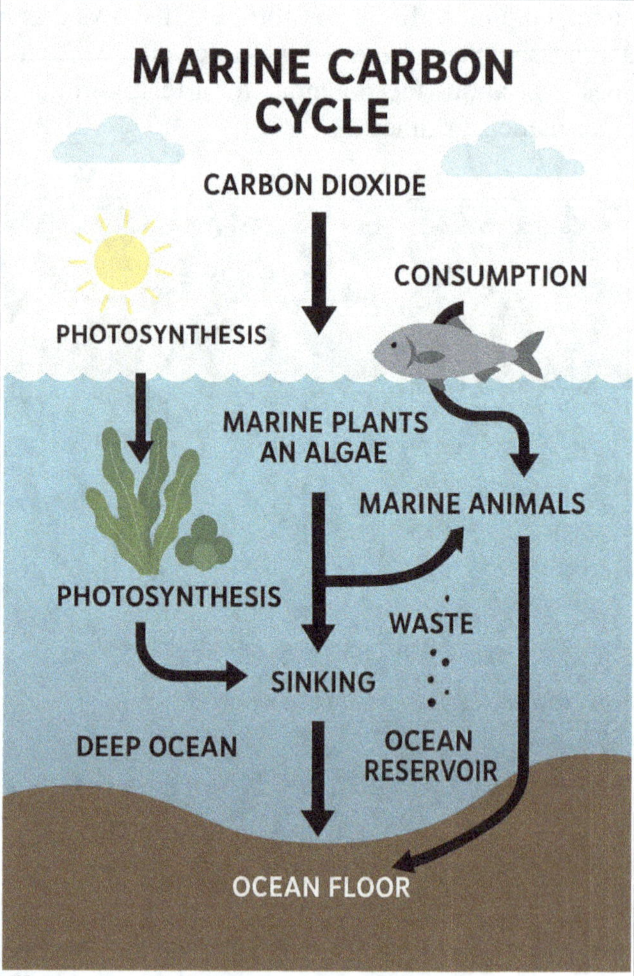

When marine animals feed on these plants, carbon enters their bodies. Some of this carbon is used for

Illustration 13: Marine carbon cycle

growth and energy, while the rest is released as waste. This waste, along with the remains of dead marine organisms, often sinks into the deeper layers of the ocean.

In the depths, carbon continues to circulate. Deep-sea creatures may feed on the falling organic material, known as marine snow, or it may settle on the ocean floor, becoming part of long-term sediment layers. Over time, the ocean floor becomes one of Earth's largest and most important carbon reservoirs, holding vast quantities of carbon in a stable form.

This storage process is important for Earth's climate. When carbon remains locked in the ocean rather than circulating in the atmosphere, it helps prevent excessive buildup of carbon dioxide. Too much atmospheric CO_2 traps heat from the sun, leading to global warming, a gradual increase in Earth's temperature that affects weather patterns, sea levels, and ecosystems worldwide.

By absorbing and storing carbon, the ocean helps to moderate Earth's climate and maintain balance in the carbon cycle. Understanding and protecting this natural process is essential for addressing climate change and preserving the health of life on Earth.

Phytoplankton: Microscopic Powerhouses of the Ocean

Phytoplankton are microscopic, plant-like organisms that float near the surface of the ocean. They include a wide variety of tiny plants, algae, and photosynthetic bacteria. Like land-based plants, phytoplankton use photosynthesis to convert sunlight, carbon dioxide and water into energy-rich compounds and oxygen. However, because photosynthesis requires sunlight, phytoplankton are restricted to the uppermost layer of the ocean, where sunlight can still penetrate, primarily in the epipelagic zone.

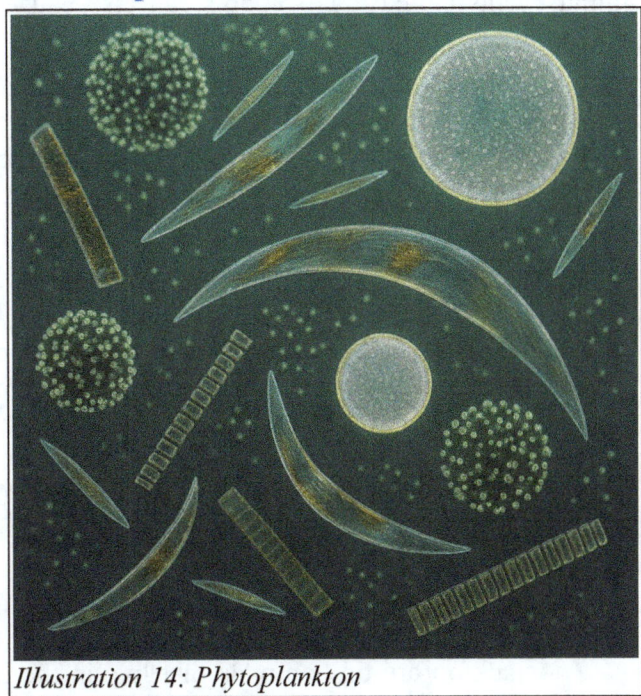

Illustration 14: Phytoplankton

Despite their small size, phytoplankton play one of the most vital roles in Earth's ecosystems. They form the foundation of the ocean's food web. When zooplankton, tiny animals that drift in the sea, consume phytoplankton, they absorb the stored energy and nutrients from the phytoplankton. These zooplankton, in turn, are eaten by larger animals, passing the energy upward through the food chain. In this way, phytoplankton make possible the incredible biodiversity of marine life, from tiny shrimp to massive whales.

Phytoplankton are found in every ocean on Earth, and though they are microscopic, their global impact is enormous. Collectively, they perform approximately half of all photosynthesis on the planet. This means they are responsible for producing a significant portion of the Earth's oxygen while simultaneously removing carbon dioxide from the atmosphere. In doing so, phytoplankton play a key role in regulating Earth's climate and slowing the effects of global warming.

Most phytoplankton are too small to be seen without the aid of a microscope. However, when they occur in large numbers, they can color the water. For example, a pond that appears green often contains a high concentration of phytoplankton, particularly types of algae. In the ocean, similar events called algal blooms can also cause changes in water color, sometimes appearing green, brown, or even red.

- There are many different types of phytoplankton, each with unique characteristics:
- Cyanobacteria – Also known as blue-green algae, these are photosynthetic bacteria that were among the first life forms on Earth.
- Diatoms – These single-celled organisms construct intricate shells made of *silica* (not calcium carbonate) that resemble glass.
- Dinoflagellates – These plankton are both photosynthetic and heterotrophic, meaning they can also consume other organisms. Some dinoflagellates are known for creating bioluminescence, emitting light in the dark ocean.

Through their role in photosynthesis, carbon cycling and as the foundation of marine food chains, phytoplankton are among the most essential and remarkable organisms on Earth, even though they are invisible without a microscope.

Zooplankton: Drifting Animals of the Ocean

Zooplankton are tiny animals that live in the ocean's waters. Most are microscopic, so small that they cannot be seen without a microscope. Because of their very small size, they have limited ability to swim and instead drift with the ocean's currents, often traveling great distances across different regions of the ocean.

Zooplankton are not all the same; they include a wide range of species and life stages of various animals. Some are single-celled protozoa, while others are the early developmental stages of larger creatures, such as crabs or fish. Unlike phytoplankton, which are capable of photosynthesis, zooplankton must feed on other organisms to survive, primarily on phytoplankton.

The distribution of zooplankton in the ocean is influenced by several factors, including temperature, salinity (the saltiness of the water), and depth. One of the most important influences on zooplankton populations is a process known as water column mixing. When deep ocean water, rich in nutrients, rises to the surface, it supports the growth of phytoplankton. As the phytoplankton population increases, so does the food supply for zooplankton. This, in turn, leads to an increase in zooplankton numbers.

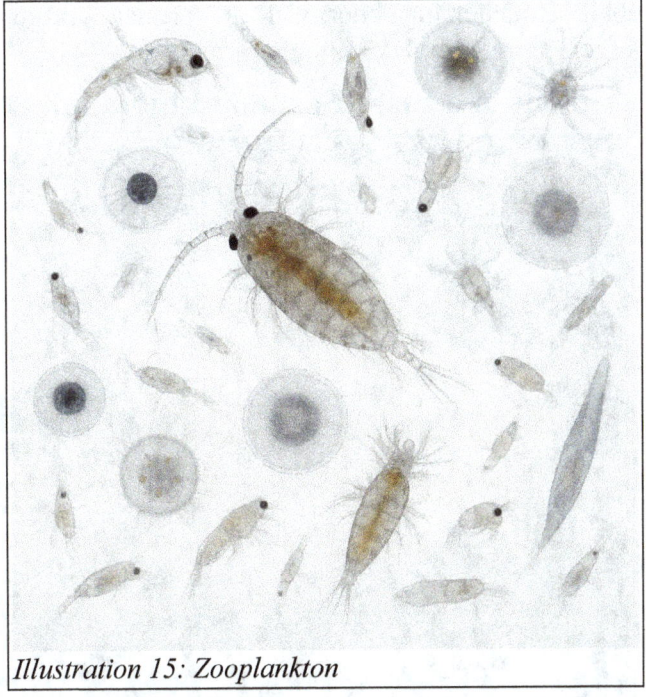
Illustration 15: Zooplankton

Because many zooplankton reproduce quickly, they can respond rapidly to changes in their environment. When phytoplankton become abundant, zooplankton populations often expand to match the available food supply. This dynamic relationship is a key part of the marine food web, linking the energy of the sun, which is captured by phytoplankton, to larger animals such as fish, whales, and seabirds that feed on zooplankton directly or indirectly.

There are many different types of zooplankton, including:
- Copepods – Tiny crustaceans that are among the most abundant animals in the ocean.
- Gastropod larvae – The early life stages of snails and other similar mollusks.
- Doliolids – Barrel-shaped animals that move by contracting their bodies.
- Fish eggs – The first stage in the life cycle of many marine fish.
- Decapod larvae – Young forms of crabs, lobsters, and shrimp, which eventually grow into larger crustaceans.

Though nearly invisible to the naked eye, zooplankton are essential to marine ecosystems. They form the critical middle link in the ocean food chain, transferring energy from primary producers (phytoplankton) to larger, more complex animals.

Parts of a Fish: Form and Function Beneath the Waves

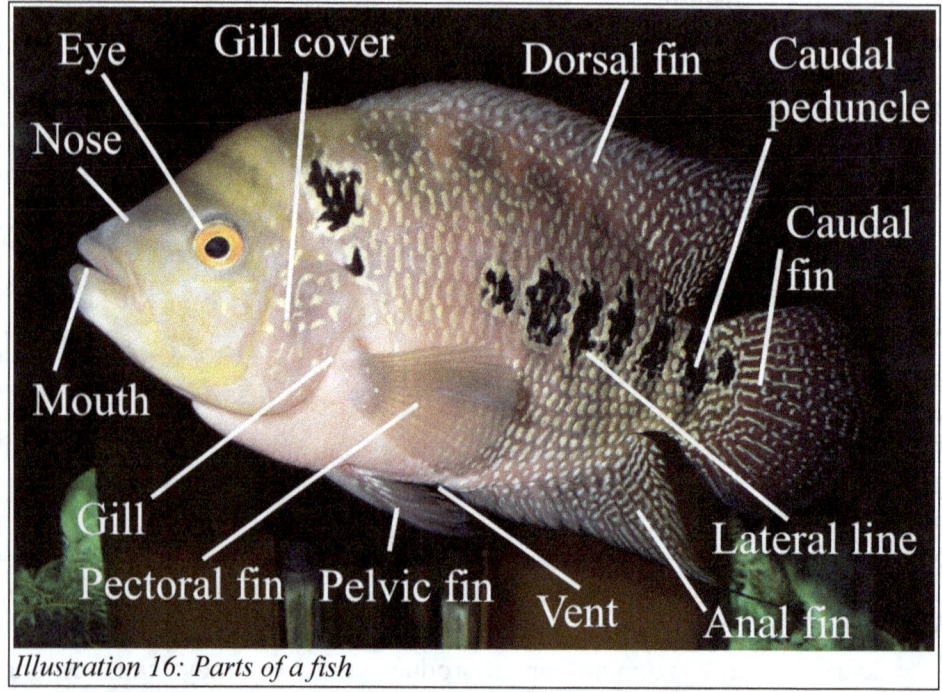

Illustration 16: Parts of a fish

While fish vary greatly in size, shape, and appearance, most share a common body structure. Although the proportions may differ, some parts being large, others quite small, their basic anatomy (shape of their body parts) follows a similar plan.

Eyes – Fish use their eyes to see, much like humans do. In the deep sea, where sunlight is nearly or completely absent, many fish have evolved unusually large or uniquely shaped eyes to help them detect the faintest traces of light. However, some deep-sea fish have poor vision or are nearly blind. These species rely on alternative sensory adaptations, such as barbels or feelers, and the lateral line system, a series of sensory cells that detect subtle vibrations and changes in water pressure, helping them sense nearby movement in the darkness.

Nostrils (Naïres) – Fish have nostrils that do not serve for breathing, but rather for detecting chemicals in the water, similar to how humans use their noses to detect odors in the air. This sense of "smell" allows them to locate food, recognize other animals, and navigate their environment.

Mouth – The mouth is used to ingest both food and water. The shape and size of the mouth determine what a fish can eat. In many deep-sea species, the mouth is extremely large, often extending beyond the head, allowing them to swallow prey whole, even animals nearly as large as themselves. This adaptation is especially useful in the deep ocean, where food can be scarce.

In contrast, some deep-sea creatures such as squid possess a beak rather than a traditional mouth. Similar to the beak of a bird, this sharp, hard structure enables them to bite and tear chunks from their prey.

Gills and Gill Covers – Behind the head, most fish have gills, specialized organs that pull oxygen from the water. A bony plate called the gill cover (or operculum) protects the gills and moves back and forth as the fish pumps water through its mouth and over the gills. Just as humans use lungs to breathe air, fish rely on gills to breathe underwater.

Fins – Most fish have five main fins, each serving a specific function:
- Dorsal fin – Located on the back, it helps the fish remain upright and stable.
- Anal fin – Found on the underside near the tail, it also aids in balance.
- Pectoral fins – Located on each side near the front, they help with steering and slow movement.
- Pelvic fins – Found on the underside, they assist in stability and maneuvering.
- Caudal fin – Commonly known as the tail fin, it provides the thrust needed for rapid swimming.

While these fins have general roles, there are exceptions. For instance, the oarfish, a long, ribbon-like deep-sea fish, swims by waving its dorsal fin rather than using its tail, an unusual but effective mode of movement.

Understanding the structure and function of these body parts helps scientists learn how fish are adapted to survive in a wide range of marine

New Wonders of the Deep (2023–2025)

Beneath the waves lies one of Earth's last great mysteries: the deep ocean. It's a realm of pitch-black darkness, crushing pressures, and creatures stranger than any alien. And guess what? The deeper we dive, the more it surprises us! Thanks to amazing new technologies and international teamwork, scientists have made thrilling new discoveries in just the past couple of years. Let's take a deep-sea dive through some of the coolest recent finds:

1. A Parade of Brand-New Creatures! (Ocean Census Initiative)
   A bold project called the Ocean Census, launched in 2023, is on a

mission to discover 100,000 new species within ten years. They're already off to a stunning start. In just two years, scientists have uncovered 866 new species! Here are some of the most fascinating:

Illustration 17: Guitar shark

- Guitar shark (an endangered and super cool shark with a flat body like a guitar!).
- Deep-sea limpet that can live in super-acidic waters (yikes!).
- Pygmy pipehorse (a tiny relative of seahorses, just 4 cm or 1.5 inches long).
- Venomous sea snails whose poisons might one day help fight pain and cancer.
- Octocorals, including the first ever found in the Maldives
- Plus: strange new sponges, shrimp, crabs, fish, sea spiders, mud dragons (yes, tiny mud dragons!), and more. Where were these new species found? All over the globe, off Mozambique, Tanzania, New Caledonia, Vanuatu, the Maldives, and even near New Zealand!

2. **The Mystery of "Dark Oxygen"**

Oxygen in the Dark? No way! For as long as anyone can remember, scientists believed that free oxygen could only be made with sunlight. But in 2025, a shocking discovery was made: oxygen is being released in total darkness, right on the ocean floor! This so-called Dark Oxygen was first found in an area called the Clarion-Clipperton Zone (between Hawaii and Mexico).

Why is this such a big deal? Well, it might change how we think life began on Earth and it hints that life could survive on other planets even without sunlight! Research is still going on, but this could be one of the most important discoveries of the decade.

3. **Baby Octopus Nurseries!**

In 2023, explorers off the coast of Costa Rica discovered something heartwarming: deep-sea octopus nurseries!

They found four new octopus species, including one named the "Dorado Octopus." These octopuses lay their eggs near hydrothermal springs, places on the seafloor where warm water gushes out. It turns out the warmth helps the octopus eggs grow, so these clever moms have adapted to brood their eggs in these cozy underwater "nurseries."

4. **Incredible New Exploration Tools**

   Exploring the deep sea is hard, but thanks to new tech, we're better at it than ever! Check this out:

   Illustration 18: Dorado octopus

   Super ROVs: New underwater robots like "Taurus" can dive 2.5 miles deep, livestream 4K video, and help scientists discover new species.

   Smarter Navigation: Underwater vehicles now use **beacons** and advanced sensors to move around precisely, even when GPS doesn't work down there!

   Laser Probes: Scientists are testing laser-equipped probes that analyze deep-sea chemistry on the spot. There's no need to bring samples to the surface.

   AI Robots for Mining: Some companies are building AI-powered robots to carefully collect metal-rich rocks from the seafloor. But beware! Deep-sea mining is controversial, and many scientists are worried about how much it would harm ocean life.

5. **How Much of the Deep Ocean Have We Mapped?**

   Brace yourself: less than 0.001% of the deep seafloor has ever been seen by human eyes or cameras! In other words, we've barely scratched the surface of what's down there.

   But exciting expeditions are ongoing! Teams from NOAA and the Ocean Exploration Trust are sending ships like the E/V Nautilus to places like:
   - Hawai'i
   - Palau
   - Guam
   - The Mariana Arc
   - Peru and Chile
   - And more mysterious regions full of methane seeps and underwater volcanoes!

The Adventure is Just Beginning!

With every dive, we learn more about this breathtaking alien world right here on our own planet. There are still countless creatures to discover and strange mysteries to solve. But one thing is clear: the deep ocean matters a lot. It plays a vital role in Earth's ecosystems, and we must protect it as we continue to explore its wonders.

Ready to dive deeper? The next great discovery might just be waiting for you!

Atlantic Hagfish: Slimemaster

Imagine a creature so strange, so wonderfully weird, that it looks like a slippery eel, oozes slime like a wizard casts spells, and eats its food from the inside out. Meet the Atlantic hagfish (*Myxine glutinosa*), a deep-sea oddball that's part mystery, part mucus, and all marvel.

Illustration 19: Atlantic hagfish protecting its eggs

This fish doesn't nibble or chew its food politely. Oh no! The hagfish has a sandpaper tongue, rough and rasping. When it finds a tasty fish (usually one that's already dead), it scrapes and grinds its way through the skin and into the body, feasting from the inside out like a sneaky dinner guest who skips the door and tunnels through the basement. Talk about unconventional dining!

But the hagfish isn't picky. Worms? Delicious. Crustaceans? Perfect snacks. And if there's nothing around to munch on, no problem. The hagfish has such a slow metabolism it can survive for months without eating a thing. It's like the ultimate deep-sea hibernator.

Unlike most fish, the Atlantic hagfish has no scales and no jaws. That's right, no jaws. Instead, it uses its gristly tongue to scrape its meals apart. And bones? Forget it. Hagfish, like sharks, are made of cartilage, that bendy, rubbery stuff in your ears and nose.

Now, let's talk slime. The hagfish is the reigning slime champion of the ocean. When threatened, it secretes (squirts out) clouds of sticky goo, so thick and fibrous that predators gag and swim away, quite literally choking on their own bad decisions. Scientists believe the slime clogs the gills of anything foolish enough to try taking a bite. One squirt, and the hagfish slips away, leaving behind a mess no vacuum cleaner could handle.

Because it lives in the mesopelagic and bathyal zones, far beneath the surface in the cold, murky waters of the North Atlantic and Arctic Oceans, its eyes aren't much help. Instead, the hagfish uses an excellent sense of smell and touch to find food buried in the mud, where it spends its days burrowing like a snotty snake with a mission.

And if all that wasn't enough to make you gasp in fascination, here's more: Baby hagfish are born with both male and female parts. A creature with both male and female parts is called a hermaphrodite. As they grow, they can switch sexes, a superpower in the deep sea! When it's time to make more hagfish, they lay about 30 eggs that stick together in a cluster like a deep-sea bouquet. Some hagfish have even been caught giving their eggs a hug, curling around them protectively in the inky dark.

People do fish for hagfish, oddly enough, not to eat them, but for their thick skin. Once dried and treated, it becomes leather sold as "eel skin." (Surprise: your wallet or purse might be a hagfish in disguise.)

So the next time someone tells you fish are boring, just whisper the words Atlantic hagfish, and watch their eyes widen in awe, or maybe a little horror. Either way, this creature is pure deep-sea wonder. Slime and all.

Barreleye: The See-Through Spectacle

Now imagine this: a fish with a clear, see-through head, eyes like green tubes pointing straight up, and a built-in flashlight in its belly. No, this isn't science fiction. Meet the barreleye (*Opisthoproctus soleatus*), a deep-sea wonder that seems more like a cartoon alien than a creature of Earth's oceans.

Illustration 20: Barreleye

Your eyes are round, right? But barreleye eyes are shaped more like barrels, which gives it its name. These tubular eyes are perfectly adapted for life in the mesopelagic zone, the twilight zone of the ocean, where only a little sunlight reaches. Instead of pointing forward like ours, the barreleye's eyes are aimed upward, like twin telescopes, constantly scanning the water above for the silhouettes of tasty snacks swimming near the surface.

Where does this oddball live? The barreleye hangs out in tropical seas around the world, though it's especially common in the Atlantic Ocean. These strange little fish only grow to about 10.5 centimeters long (that's just over 4 inches), and they drift quietly at depths of 500 to 700 meters (1,600 to 2,300 feet), a place where it's always dim, cold, and mysterious.

But wait! It gets even weirder!

Inside its belly, the barreleye hosts glowing bacteria. Yes, glowing! These bioluminescent bacteria produce light from within the fish, and the barreleye has a clever little mirror tucked inside to direct that glow downward. The light shines out through a special translucent patch on the fish's underside in a sneaky trick called counterillumination. To any predator lurking below, the barreleye seems to vanish, blending in with the faint glow from above. It's like invisibility, deep-sea style!

And what's on the menu for a barreleye? Mostly siphonophores, jelly-like animals that link together in long, wiggly chains like underwater necklaces. These chains can stretch for meters, and the barreleye carefully plucks its prey from the drifting strands.

So the next time someone tells you the deep sea is empty or dull, tell them about the barreleye. It's a fish with a transparent dome-head, barrel-shaped eyes that swivel under glass, glowing belly-lights, and stealth-mode camouflage. In the great theater of the ocean, the barreleye is part mystery, part marvel, and 100% deep-sea drama.

Black Swallower: Eats Fish Larger Than Itself

Imagine if you could gulp down something twice your height and ten times your weight. Say… an entire alligator? Sounds like a recipe for disaster, right? But for the black swallower (*Chiasmodon niger*), that's just dinner.

This deep-sea marvel doesn't nibble or chew. Nope. It swallows its prey whole. And not just any prey. It eats bony fish that are sometimes double its length and ten times heavier! If you were a black swallower, that would be like slurping down a three-meter-long, 450-kilogram alligator in one go. Yikes.

But how does a fish no longer than your foot manage such an outrageous feat? That's still a mystery. No one has ever seen a black

Illustration 21: Black swallower

swallower mid-meal. One scientist, Theodore Gill, had a theory: maybe the swallower grabs the tail and slowly works its way forward, gulp by gulp. With a mouth that opens wider than its own head and rows of needle-sharp teeth, it's built for gripping and gulping. Other scientists think it might sneak up, chomp down on the head, wait for the fish to suffocate… then gobble it up.

But here's the catch. Sometimes, the black swallower bites off more than it can Rotting produces gas, turning the black swallower into a bloated balloon. It floats helplessly up to the surface, where it usually dies. In fact, that's how many scientists have found black swallowers, swollen and floating, victims of their own epic appetites.

One poor fish was found dead at just 19 centimeters (7.4 inches) long… with a massive 86-centimeter (34-inch) snake mackerel stuffed inside its belly. That's almost like a hamster trying to eat a Great Dane!

Black swallowers grow up to about 25 centimeters (10 inches) long and live in warm seas near the equator. Think the Atlantic, Pacific, and Indian Oceans. You'll find them lurking in the mesopelagic and bathypelagic zones, far below the reach of sunlight.

They have long, skinny bodies with no scales and dark brownish-black skin, perfect for blending into the deep. Their babies start life near the ocean's surface as tiny, floating eggs. Once hatched, the larvae are completely on their own. As they grow, they dive deeper and deeper into the dark, secret world of the deep sea.

So the next time you eat a big meal and say, "I couldn't eat another bite," remember the black swallower, who probably could… and just might regret it.

Blobfish: A Gelatinous Mass

Illustration 22: Blobfish

They say, "Beauty is in the eye of the beholder." Well, behold: the blobfish! With a face like a melting scoop of pink pudding and a body that looks like it lost an argument with gravity, the blobfish (genus *Psychrolutes*) might just win the title of the ocean's most misunderstood creature.

But don't let its sad, squishy looks fool you. This gelatinous wonder is a deep-sea survival expert. Blobfish live in the bathyal zone, the dark, crushing depths of the ocean, where the water pressure is up to 80 times greater than at the surface. If you were down there without a deep-sea sub, you'd be squished like a pancake. But the blobfish? It's perfectly built for this life.

Instead of bones and muscles like many other fish, the blobfish's body is mostly goo. Yup. Think of it like a living jelly mold. That soft body is just a little less dense than the surrounding water, which lets it hover effortlessly above the ocean floor. No swimming is required, just a gentle float, like a ghost of the sea.

And since food is scarce down there, the blobfish doesn't waste energy chasing prey. It's the ultimate couch potato of the deep sea. It drifts silently just above the seabed, waiting. If something delicious such as a crab or a sea pen crawls or floats by, the blobfish opens its mouth and gulp, down the hatch it goes! No chasing. No chewing. Just snack and float.

Blobfish grow to about 30 centimeters (12 inches) in length, about the size of a school ruler. But they've gained internet fame for something totally unfair: what they look like when they're taken out of the water. At the surface, without the intense pressure of the deep sea holding their shape, their bodies collapse into a squishy blob. That's why they look so droopy in photos. Down where they live, though, they actually look more like regular fish. They're still squishy, sure, but less like a sad balloon.

So next time someone makes fun of the blobfish, just remember: it's perfectly adapted to one of the most extreme environments on Earth. It's not ugly. It's awesome.

Bluefin Tuna: A Warm Blooded Fish

Illustration 23: Bluefin Tuna

If the ocean had superheroes, the bluefin tuna would be wearing a cape. This mighty fish doesn't just hang out in one part of the sea. It zooms up and down through the ocean's layers in a super-swim called vertical migration. From chilly deep waters of the upper part of the Mesopelagic Zone to sunlit surfaces of the Epipelagic Zone, the bluefin tuna (*genus Thunnus*) is always on the move.

And what a fish it is! The biggest bluefin tuna can grow over 3 meters (nearly 10 feet) long and weigh up to 450 kilograms (990 pounds), about the same as a grand piano. That's no goldfish.

But what truly makes the bluefin tuna a marvel of the sea is that it's warm-blooded. Most fish are cold-blooded, which means their body temperature matches the water around them. But the bluefin tuna? It's like a portable furnace. It can heat itself up, giving it a big advantage. Warmer muscles mean faster swimming, sharper senses, and longer journeys in search of food.

Of course, there's a catch. Making body heat takes a ton of energy, so the bluefin tuna needs to eat a lot. It's not picky: fish, squids, shrimp, you name it. If it moves and it fits in the tuna's mouth, it's on the menu.

Now here's something wild: bluefin tuna must keep swimming nonstop. Why? Because swimming pushes water over their gills, helping them breathe. If they ever stop, they suffocate. Seriously. That's why their gills are supercharged, with seven times more surface area than those of a typical fish. These gills are mega oxygen-collecting machines.

But as amazing as they are, bluefin tuna are in trouble. Their meat is so prized, especially in sushi, that they've been overfished nearly to the brink of extinction. The Atlantic bluefin tuna, in particular, has taken a huge hit. Some of the biggest ones ever caught weighed over 680 kilograms (1,500 pounds). That's more than a horse!

Luckily, there's hope. In places like Australia, people are now farming bluefin tuna. These "ocean ranches" harvest between 7,000 and 10,000 tonnes a year, helping protect wild populations.

There are four known species of bluefin tuna, and here's your quick dive into each:

- Southern Bluefin Tuna (*Thunnus maccoyii*) Found in the oceans of the southern hemisphere. Grows up to 2.5 meters (8.2 feet) and weighs as much as 260 kilograms (570 pounds).
- Pacific Bluefin Tuna (*Thunnus orientalis*) Swims through the northern Pacific and parts of the southern Pacific. Can reach up to 3 meters (9.8 feet) and 450 kilograms (990 pounds).
- Atlantic Bluefin Tuna (*Thunnus thynnus*) Roams both sides of the Atlantic Ocean and the Mediterranean Sea. The true giants of the family. Some tip the scales at 680 kilograms (1,500 pounds).
- Longtail Tuna (*Thunnus tonggol*) Sometimes included in the bluefin family. Smaller than the others, but still a speedy swimmer of warm coastal waters.

So, next time you think of tuna, don't picture a sandwich. Picture a sleek, muscle-powered, warm-blooded ocean rocket. The bluefin tuna is built for adventure, born to roam, and constantly racing the currents of the sea.

Blue Goo: What Are You?

Imagine you're a scientist, exploring the inky darkness of the deep sea with a robot camera. Suddenly, on the ocean floor, you spot something weird. It's blue. It's gooey. And it's alive.

In 2022, while cruising through the Caribbean Sea, researchers aboard NOAA's exploration ship *Okeanos Explorer* made just such a discovery. At around 1,400 feet deep in the bathyal zone, they came across a mysterious blob. Not just one, but a whole gathering of them, scattered across the seafloor like little alien jelly drops. Scientists jokingly nicknamed them "blue goo."

But what is blue goo? Here's the fun part: no one knows. Not yet, anyway.

The blue goo blobs didn't match anything scientists had seen before. Were they soft corals? Maybe sponges? Or could they be tunicates, strange sea creatures also known as sea squirts? No one could say for sure. It was like nature dropped a riddle in the deep sea and dared humanity to solve it.

This is how scientific discovery often begins, with

Illustration 24: Blue goo

mystery. First, something strange is spotted. If researchers are lucky, they collect a specimen (which is trickier than it sounds in pitch-black water, under crushing pressure, using robotic arms!). Then, the real detective work starts.

Scientists study the creature's shape and structure, looking for clues. If they get a sample, they can even test its DNA, like running a biological fingerprint, to see how it fits on the giant family tree of life. Sometimes it takes years to figure out what a new creature is, and whether it's truly new to science or just a rare version of something already known.

In the case of blue goo, the blobs haven't officially been identified yet. They might turn out to be something familiar or something completely new, never before seen by human eyes. Either way, they're a reminder that Earth still holds secrets, especially in the deep sea, which remains one of the most unexplored frontiers on the planet.

So next time you think science has discovered everything, remember the blue goo. Down in the dark, there are still creatures waiting to be found, shiny, slimy, and wonderfully unknown.

Bluntnose Sixgill Shark: Sibling Rivalry to the Max

Sibling rivalry can be rough. Just imagine if it ended with your brother or sister eating you. That's not a joke. It's just how life begins for the bluntnose sixgill shark (*Hexanchus griseus*), one of the ocean's most ancient and mysterious creatures.

Inside a mother sixgill shark, dozens of tiny shark embryos begin to grow, sometimes more than 100 at once! At first, these developing pups

Illustration 25: Bluntnose sixgill shark

feed on leftover, unfertilized eggs. But soon, they turn on each other. In a dark underwater nursery inside their mother, the strongest pups eat their weaker siblings, one bite at a time. It's survival of the hungriest.

When these fierce little sharks are finally born, each one is already around 70 centimeters long. That's over 2 feet of pure determination. And even though they've had a brutal start, they often grow up near the same place they were born, swimming alongside the brothers and sisters they didn't eat. Scientists at the Seattle Aquarium discovered this using DNA testing. This is like a deep-sea version of a family reunion.

The bluntnose sixgill shark has many names. Some people call it the cow shark (for its rounded snout), or the mud shark (since it loves the ocean's murky bottom). But whatever you call it, you're looking at a living fossil. This shark's ancient relatives were already prowling the seas 200 million years ago, back when dinosaurs ruled the land. The sixgill has survived mass extinctions, ice ages, and dramatic changes in Earth's oceans and it's still here.

These sharks can grow up to 5.4 meters long. That's a whopping 18 feet, which is longer than most cars. Most adults average around 4.8 meters (or 16 feet). Their skin color ranges from muddy tan to midnight black, and their eyes glow a ghostly green thanks to a trick of light called fluorescence. They're found in oceans all over the world, from chilly polar waters to warm tropical seas.

Despite their fearsome start in life, adult sixgill sharks tend to be slow movers. They cruise along the seafloor, sometimes over a mile deep, in water that's icy cold and pitch-black. During the day, they stay deep, anywhere between 90 and 1,800 meters down, mainly in

Illustration 26: Lower jaw and teeth of a male bluntnose shark

the bathyal zone, but have been found deep as the abyssal zone. But when the sun goes down, they rise into the epipelagic zone, hunting in the twilight like ancient shadowy ghosts.

And what's on the menu for a sixgill shark? Almost anything it can catch! Fish, squid, crustaceans, even the occasional seal or smaller shark. They are not picky eaters, which helps them flourish in oceans all around the planet.

Mating season can be wild. Male sixgill sharks are believed to bite the females near their gills, with those six rows of razor-sharp teeth, to convince them to mate. Let's just say, romance in the deep sea is a lot more intense than just flowers and chocolates.

It's no wonder these sharks are loners, swimming through the deep in silence and mystery, reminders of a time when the world was ruled by giants.

Chambered Nautilus: A Spit Machine

Can *you* spit so hard you go flying backward? Probably not, and please don't try it at the dinner table. But the chambered nautilus (*Nautilus pompilius*) has mastered the art of spit propulsion. Spit propulsion is not only cool, it's how it swims.

Using a clever built-in funnel called a siphon, the nautilus slurps in water and then blasts it out with a powerful squirt. That burst of water

Illustration 27: Chambered nautilus

pushes the nautilus in the opposite direction, just like a balloon zooming around when you let go of it. It might not win any races, but it can jet along at about 1 meter per second (that's 3 feet per second.) That's pretty impressive for a shelled explorer!

The chambered nautilus is part of an elite group of ocean animals called cephalopods, which includes brainy squid, sneaky cuttlefish, and the ultra-flexible octopus. But unlike its squishier cousins, the nautilus comes with its own built-in armor, a fabulous, spiraled shell.

Now, let's talk tentacles. You have two arms. The nautilus? Around ninety! These tentacles are sticky and groovy, perfect for grabbing food and exploring rocky nooks on the ocean floor. Instead of seeing or hearing food, it smells with its tentacles. It's like sniffing your dinner with your fingers. Once it finds a tasty morsel, maybe a crab, a small fish, or even the cast-off shell of something that molted, it uses its parrot-like beak to crunch it to bits.

Illustration 28: Chambered Nautilus Beak

By day, the chambered nautilus dives down deep into the mesopelagic zone, 275 to 600 meters (up to 2,000 feet) below the surface. It rests in the cold, dark depths like a coiled mystery. But by night, it rises up to shallower waters of the epipelagic zone, cruising between 90 and 150 meters (about 300 to 500 feet). It spits its way in search of dinner. It's like the ocean's version of a nighttime snacker.

And now for its secret superpower: built-in buoyancy control. The nautilus's shell is made of chambers. When it hatches, it starts with about four chambers. As it grows, it adds more, like building extra rooms onto a spiraled house. To float, it fills these chambers with gas. To dive, it floods them with water. It's basically operating like a tiny submarine that is alive!

But even submarines have enemies. Sharks and octopuses like to snack on nautiluses. When danger comes, the nautilus pulls its soft body inside its shell and seals the entrance with a leathery hood, like slamming the door shut. Still, some predators are strong enough to crack the shell and gobble the soft bits inside.

Nautilus shells are beautifully striped with creamy white and rusty orange patches. Humans have been collecting them for centuries. Unfortunately, too many are being taken from the ocean, and that worries scientists and environmentalists. These creatures don't grow fast, and their numbers are slowly shrinking. They're treasures of the sea, but we have to let them live if we want them to stick around.

Did you know the chambered nautilus is a living fossil? Its family tree goes back 400 million years, a full 265 million years before the first dinosaurs stomped the Earth. At one point, the oceans teemed with over 10,000 different kinds of nautiluses. Now, only a few remain.

They are the time travelers of the deep. Mystery mollusks wrapped in spirals of ancient wonder, still gliding through the sea with a quiet whoosh.

Coelacanth: Master of Chill

Illustration 29: Coelacanth

Imagine a fish from 350 million years ago, back when giant dragonflies buzzed above fern forests and the continents were still deciding where to go. Now imagine that fish is still swimming today. Meet the coelacanth (say: *SEE-luh-kanth*), (*Latimeria chalumnae*) one of the oldest surviving species of fish on Earth. It is a true time traveler of the sea!

How has the coelacanth survived for so long without a single fashion update? One big secret: it's a master of chill. When food is scarce, it slows its metabolism way down. Metabolism is how fast your body burns through the energy from your food. The coelacanth is the ocean's energy-saving expert. No snack? No problem. It can survive on just a little.

Its diet? Squid, eels, and other slippery snacks of the sea. But don't expect chewing. The coelacanth doesn't nibble or bite. It gulps. Its jaw is hinged at the back of its skull, like a trapdoor. When prey gets close enough, *whoosh!*, it opens its mouth wide and swallows its meal whole.

Coelacanths grow big, up to 2 meters (6 feet) long and around 80 kilograms (176 pounds). Their deep ocean blue color helps them blend into the shadows of the sea. And here's a weird-but-true fact: their head is mostly fat. Their brain? Tiny. Like, peanut-sized. So yes, calling a coelacanth a "fathead" would technically be accurate (but kind of rude).

They don't rush into adulthood either. Coelacanths don't have babies until they're about 20 years old. And unlike most fish, they don't lay eggs. Nope. Baby coelacanths, called pups, are born alive! A mother might have 5 to 25 of them at once. And guess what? From the moment they're born, the pups are on their own. No bedtime stories. Just, "Here's the ocean. Good luck!"

They are deep-sea dwellers, usually found in the mesopelagic zone, 90 to 200 meters (about 300 to 650 feet) below the surface, off the coasts of Africa and Indonesia. They prefer chilly water because their gills breathe better in the cold, Kind of like how we breathe easier in fresh mountain air.

And here's a showstopper: Coelacanths don't always swim forward. Sometimes they cruise backward. And, sometimes upside down. Scientists think this helps them sneak up on prey. Coelacanths are like the acrobats of the abyss!

For a long time, people thought they were extinct. They were known only from fossils. Then, in 1938, a fisherman caught a real, live coelacanth off the coast of South Africa. Scientists were stunned. When another one turned up in 1952, they practically threw a party.

Today, scientists think there are only about 500 coelacanths left in the wild. That makes them endangered and precious. Every single one is a living window into a world long gone. They've seen the rise of dinosaurs, the fall of empires, and now, the rise of curious teens like you.

So next time someone asks what creature has barely changed in hundreds of millions of years, you can grin and say: "Oh, you mean the coelacanth? My favorite ancient, backward-swimming, fat-headed gulp-monster?"

Cookiecutter Shark: The Bite-Sized Terror

Illustration 30: Cookiecutter shark

You've probably seen a cookie cutter in your kitchen, the kind that punches out perfect little shapes from rolled dough. But have you ever heard of a cookiecutter shark? This deep-sea creature doesn't cut cookies. It cuts creatures. It chomps perfect circles of flesh from whales, fish, and even submarines (yes, really). No baking required! Just bite and gulp!

The cookiecutter shark (*Isistius brasiliensis*) is a sneaky little predator, growing only about 50 centimeters long (just under 2 feet). But don't let its small size fool you. It's got one of the nastiest bites in the deep! These sharks spend their days in the deep, dark parts of the ocean, the mesopelagic zone from 1,000 to 3,700 meters (that's up to 12,100 feet deep!). At night, they creep upward to about 85 meters (around 280 feet) to hunt for dinner in the epipelagic zone.

How does it take a bite that looks like it was cut with a cookie cutter? With teeth like tiny saw blades! First, the shark sticks to its victim using suction-cup lips. Then it sinks its jagged lower teeth into the flesh and spins in a circle, like a bite-sized buzzsaw. When it's done, it leaves behind a neat, circular wound about the size of a ping pong ball. Ouch!

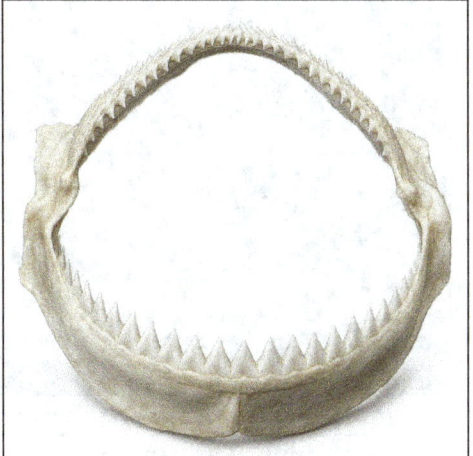

Illustration 31: Cookiecutter Shark Teeth

But that's not the only weird trick up its fin. The cookiecutter shark glows! Its belly is covered in green photophores. Photophores are cells that give off light. This glow helps the shark hide by blending in with the faint light coming from above, a camouflage trick called counterillumination.

But wait! This shark takes counterillumination to the next level. Right in the middle of its glowing underside, it has a small dark patch shaped like a fish. Scientists think that this shadowy "fake fish" lures in big fish and bam! The cookiecutter shark strikes with its famous bite.

Do they ever bite humans? Almost never. Cookiecutter sharks live far from where most people swim. But one unlucky swimmer in the Pacific Ocean got chomped more than once! He made it back to his kayak with several cookie-shaped souvenirs taken from his legs. Yikes!

Oh, and get this. When a cookiecutter shark loses a tooth, it doesn't let it go to waste. It swallows its old teeth to recycle the calcium and grow new ones. That's deep-sea efficiency at its finest.

So next time you're baking cookies, take a second to imagine a tiny shark, glowing green in the dark, spiraling through the sea and taking perfect little bites. Sweet? Not exactly. But totally unforgettable.

Cuvier's Beaked Whale: The Deep Diving Champion!

Illustration 32: Cuvier's beaked whale

If you think you can hold your breath for a long time, try beating a Cuvier's beaked whale! These incredible whales are the current champions of deep diving among mammals. They can dive nearly 3,000 meters (almost 10,000 feet) deep and stay underwater for more than three hours! Yes, you read that right! Three hours! That's longer than it takes to watch a movie!

But let's back up a bit. What exactly is a Cuvier's beaked whale? First of all, it's not the most famous whale out there. It's not as big as a blue whale, nor as noisy as a humpback. In fact, Cuvier's beaked whales (*Ziphius cavirostris*) are pretty shy. They live far offshore in the open ocean (the pelagic zone), and they like to stay deep beneath the waves. That makes them a bit mysterious. There's a lot scientists don't know about them yet.

Cuvier's beaked whales grow to about 5 to 7 meters long (that's roughly the length of a school bus), and they weigh up to 3,000 kilograms (6,600 pounds). Their bodies are shaped like sleek torpedoes which is perfect for diving deep. They have a short, stubby beak (that's where the "beaked whale" part of their name comes from), and their skin can be various shades of gray, brown, or reddish. Older whales often have lots of white scars, probably from battles with squid (their favorite food) or from encounters with other whales.

Speaking of food, why dive so deep? Well, the tastiest squid don't hang out near the surface. Cuvier's beaked whales hunt in the bathypelagic zone, also known as the midnight zone, where sunlight never reaches. It's dark, cold, and under immense pressure down there. But Cuvier's beaked whales are perfectly adapted for it.

When they dive, their heart rate slows waaay down to save oxygen. Blood flows mostly to the brain and heart while their muscles rely on stored oxygen. They can also collapse parts of their lungs to avoid problems caused by the intense pressure. That's how they manage such record-breaking dives. Scientists recorded one dive lasting 3 hours and 42 minutes!

After a long dive, they return to the surface to breathe and rest. You might see them floating quietly, catching their breath before heading down again. Since they're so shy and dive so deep, spotting a Cuvier's beaked whale is a rare treat for ocean explorers.

In recent years, scientists have used tags to learn more about these elusive animals. Every new discovery about them leaves us amazed. How do they handle such cold? How do they navigate in total darkness? What other secrets are they hiding in the depths?

So next time you're trying to set a new personal record for holding your breath, remember the mighty Cuvier's beaked whale, the deepest diver of all whales, quietly slipping through the dark heart of the sea!

Deep Sea Anglerfish: A Light in the Dark

How big of a meal could you gulp down whole? A cheeseburger? A whole pizza? The deep sea anglerfish laughs at that. It can swallow a fish twice its size in one massive bite. That's like you swallowing a full-grown adult in a single gulp!

These bizarre beasts belong to the family *Ceratiidae* and haunt the deep ocean, living at crushing depths of the bathypelagic zone, 1,000 to 2,000 meters (3,300 to 6,500 feet).

Illustration 33: Anglerfish

Down there, it's pitch black and food is scarce. But anglerfish have a bright idea, literally. On their foreheads, they grow a glowing lure like a spooky fishing rod, which they wiggle around to tempt other fish.

This eerie glow is thanks to bioluminescence. Bioluminescence is light made by living things. Fireflies do it. Some jellyfish do it. And the anglerfish? It gets help from special glowing bacteria. The fish feeds the bacteria, and in return, the bacteria provide the haunting headlight. This teamwork is called symbiosis, and in the deep sea, it's a brilliant survival trick.

When a curious fish comes in for a closer look at the glowing lure… SNAP! The anglerfish launches forward and gulps it down whole. Its mouth can open enormously wide, and its teeth point backwards towards its stomach. So, once dinner is in, there's no getting out.

Most anglerfish look like creepy, bloated balloons with jagged teeth. They're definitely not built for speed. So instead of chasing their meals, they play the waiting game, hovering still in the gloom like underwater monsters holding lanterns.

There are over 200 species of anglerfish, most living far below the surface. And here's a strange twist: the females are giants compared to the males. A male anglerfish is tiny. So tiny, in fact, that once he finds a female, he bites her and never lets go. Over time, his body fuses with hers. He becomes part of her, living off her blood like a deep-sea vampire sidekick. He gives up his independence, but he's always there when she needs him to fertilize her eggs. When males and females are a lot different, it's called sexual dimorphism.

And oh, the eggs! A female anglerfish can lay a floating sheet of eggs up to one meter wide and nine meters long (that's 3 feet wide and 30 feet long). These eggs drift up to the sunlit surface, where the larvae hatch and snack on tiny plankton. Once they're big enough, they make the long journey back down into the inky deep, ready to glow and gulp like their parents.

Believe it or not, some people actually eat anglerfish, They say it tastes like lobster. But don't expect to see one in your local fish market. These creatures are built for the bottom, where monsters still lurk in the dark.

Deep Sea Coral: Nature's Deep Sea Art

What has branches like a plant, but is really made of tiny animals? Corals! You may have seen colorful coral reefs in shallow, tropical waters, where sunlight filters down and sea creatures dart through the coral like guests at an underwater party. But did you know there's a whole other world of coral lurking in the deep?

Illustration 34: Deep sea coral

Meet the deep sea corals, also known as cold water corals. These mysterious creatures live far below the sunlit surface, anywhere from 45 meters (150 feet) all the way down to 3,000 meters (10,000 feet). That's a world of icy darkness, where the pressure is high and the light is long gone. And yet, even in this shadowy realm, life finds a way to build beauty.

Corals are not plants. They're colonies of tiny animals called polyps, each one no bigger than a grain of rice. These polyps work together to build intricate skeletons, like little stonemasons of the sea. Shallow-water corals form rocky reefs, but deep sea corals grow into strange and wonderful shapes, feathery fans, tree-like towers, spiraling columns, and even wispy whips that can stretch over 7 meters (24 feet) tall!

Imagine something growing that big, and then picture this: It takes hundreds, even thousands of years to get there. That's because deep sea corals grow very slowly, just a few millimeters (less than half an inch) a year. Some corals found by scientists are over 1,000 years old. They are like ancient guardians of the deep.

Unlike their tropical cousins, deep sea corals don't need sunlight. They are filter feeders. They survive by filtering nutrients drifting in the cold ocean currents. These corals tend to grow in thickets, like underwater forests, and they play a vital role in deep sea ecosystems. Many creatures such as tiny shrimp, young fish, and mysterious invertebrates hide among their branches, safe from hungry predators and strong currents. When a coral provides shelter for other animals, it is called habitat-forming meaning that it creates a habitat for other creatures.

But deep sea corals face serious threats. Fishing methods like bottom trawling, which drag huge nets along the ocean floor, can crush coral forests in minutes. Laying underwater cables for internet and communication can also break apart these delicate habitats. And because they grow so slowly, damaged coral structures may take centuries to recover, if they recover at all.

Despite the danger, deep sea corals are everywhere. They're hidden in the dark, quiet corners of every ocean on Earth. They grow on underwater mountains called seamounts, rising like secret cities from the seafloor. And though they may be out of sight, they are essential to the creatures live in the deep.

So the next time you think of coral, don't just picture bright reefs in sunny shallows. Picture ancient coral towers swaying gently in the pitch-black deep, where strange animals whisper through underwater forests, and time moves ever so slowly.

Deep Sea Dragonfish: Terrors of the Deep

Illustration 35: Deep sea dragonfish

When you hear the word dragon, what comes to mind? Fire? Fangs? Ferocious roars? If you imagine a scaly creature with wicked teeth and a spooky glow, you might just be thinking of the deep sea dragonfish (*Grammatostomias flagellibarba*) a real-life monster of the midnight zone.

This pint-sized predator may only be about 15 centimeters (6 inches) long, but what it lacks in size, it makes up for in terror. The last thing many unfortunate sea creatures ever feel is the dragonfish's fearsome mouth full of needle-sharp teeth rushing through of the darkness.

The dragonfish is a stealthy hunter. Like its creepy cousin, the anglerfish, it uses a bioluminescent lure, a glowing whisker called a barbel, to attract prey. This barbel dangles from its chin like a glowing fishing line. The dragonfish flicks it on and off, wiggling it like a juicy snack. When an unlucky fish or crustacean swims in for a nibble… CHOMP! Dinner is served.

Its teeth are something out of a nightmare. They're long, clear, and some are hinged, meaning they can fold backward like trapdoors. This allows prey to slide down its throat, but not climb back up. If that wasn't enough, the dragonfish has a second set of jaws hidden deeper in its throat, ready to clamp down and finish the job. Once you're caught by a dragonfish, there's no escape! It's like an underwater horror movie in slow motion.

But even monsters have their problems. Many of the dragonfish's meals, tiny shrimp and glowing fish, are bioluminescent too. That means their light could shine through the dragonfish's see-through body, lighting it up like a glow stick for bigger predators to see. Yikes! Luckily, the dragonfish has a genius solution: a black stomach that works like a curtain, blocking all that telltale light from escaping. Secret snacks, safe from prying eyes.

Dragonfish live in the deep sea in the mesopelagic zone and the bathypelagic zone, between 1,000 and 3,000 meters (about 3,000 to 10,000 feet, or up to 2 miles deep). That's far below the reach of sunlight and very hard for scientists to explore. So, we still don't know exactly how they meet, mingle, or fall in love. But we do know this: after the female lays her eggs and the male fertilizes them, the egg raft floats to the surface. The tiny larvae hatch and grow up near the top of the ocean, before diving back into the deep when they're ready to become mini-monsters themselves.

Sound scary? Don't worry. Despite their name and terrifying tools, deep sea dragonfish are harmless to humans. They're more like mini dragons with glowsticks than sea serpents from your worst dreams.

But deep in the ocean, where the light fades and the pressure crushes, the dragonfish rules with jaws of doom and a twinkle in its chin.

Dumbo Octopus: Flappy Eared Wonder

What sea creature looks like it just flopped out of a cartoon? Meet the dumbo octopus (Genus: *Grimpoteuthi*)! With giant ear-like fins that flap like wings, this deep-sea darling gets its name from Disney's Dumbo the elephant. But instead of flying through the air, the dumbo octopus glides gracefully through the inky ocean with those fluttery fins.

There are many types of dumbo octopuses, and they live all over the world, but not anywhere you can swim to! These gentle creatures hang out way down deep in the bathypelagic zone and abyssopelagic zones, between 1,000 and 7,000 meters (up to 23,000 feet!) beneath the waves. In fact, in 2020, one was spotted floating along the bottom of the Java Trench, nearly 7,000 meters down. That's like stacking 21 Empire State Buildings on top of each other… underwater!

To stay safe from hungry predators, dumbo octopuses have a color-changing trick up their sleeves (or rather, in their skin). Special cells called chromatophores can switch their colors like magic: red, white, pink, brown, or even ocean-floor camouflage!

What's on the menu for this deep-sea drifter? Tasty treats like worms, shrimp-like crustaceans, tiny shellfish, and copepods. Scientists think they've seen dumbo octopuses hunting: the octopus floats down gently, spreads out its arms like a blanket, and wraps up its dinner in a cozy, tentacled hug.

Illustration 36: Dumbo octopus

They're clever movers, too. They squirt water out of a siphon like a tiny underwater jet, zooming along in short bursts. The ear-fins help steer and keep them steady. And their tentacles? They're multitool marvels. Perfect for crawling on the seafloor, catching snacks, laying eggs, and even poking around new places. One thing they don't do? Squirt ink. Unlike many of their octopus cousins, the dumbo octopus is ink-free!

Look closely (if you ever get the chance!) and you'll spot little translucent (see-through) patches near their eyes. These help them detect even the faintest light in the pitch-black depths.

And when it's time to make more dumbo octopuses? There's no set season. Dumbo octopuses can mate any time. The male gives the female a packet of sperm, and she saves it until the moment is just right. Once her eggs are fertilized, she carefully carries them until she finds the perfect place to leave them, like a devoted, deep-sea mom.

Just like fish, these flappy wonders breathe through gills. And while they may live in the darkest places on Earth, the dumbo octopus brings a splash of magic to the ocean's deepest mysteries.

Fangtooth: Tiny Terror with a Giant Bite

Illustration 37: Fangtooth

Would you climb a skyscraper every night just to grab a snack? That's what some fangtooth fish do, sort of! These deep-sea creatures spend their days lurking in the chilly darkness of the mesopelagic zone about 2,000 meters (6,500 feet) below the ocean's surface. But at night, they may make an epic journey upward to hunt in shallower waters. It's like taking the world's longest elevator ride just for dinner! This is called vertical migration.

Let's talk teeth. The fangtooth (*Anoplogaster cornuta*) has seriously big chompers. How big? If *you* were a fangtooth, your bottom teeth would reach from your lip all the way up to your forehead! Luckily, the fangtooth has special holes in its upper jaw to tuck those teeth into when it closes its mouth. Otherwise, it would be walking around with its mouth hanging open all the time!

Unlike you and me, the fangtooth doesn't chew. It opens wide, really wide, and swallows its prey whole. It uses its teeth more like grappling hooks to hold slippery snacks until it gulps them down. Yum?

Despite its ferocious face, the fangtooth is actually pretty small. The bigger species grows to just 15 centimeters (6 inches). That's about the width of your outstretched hand. The smaller ones only reach 10 centimeters (4 inches). But with its huge teeth and slimy, bumpy face, it has earned the nickname **ogrefish**. Sounds scary? It kind of looks like a deep-sea goblin with a bad attitude, but in a cute, fishy sort of way.

These spooky swimmers usually live between 200 and 2,000 meters (600 to 6,500 feet) deep. But they've been found as deep as 5,000 meters (16,000 feet). Down there, it's darker than midnight in a cave with no flashlight, and definitely no pizza delivery.

Because it's so dark, the fangtooth doesn't rely much on sight. In fact, its eyes aren't very useful at all. Instead, it uses a special trick called a lateral line. This is a row of tiny sensors along its body that feels vibrations in the water, like sonar in a submarine. These signals help the fangtooth find prey to munch and avoid anything that might munch it.

When baby fangtooths hatch, they look like completely different creatures. They have big eyes, spiky heads, and something called gill rakers, which help them filter tiny critters from the water. These little ones stay near the surface, growing quietly until they're about 8 centimeters (3 inches) long. Then, they head down, down, down into the deep, where they grow up into the ultimate tiny terrors of the sea.

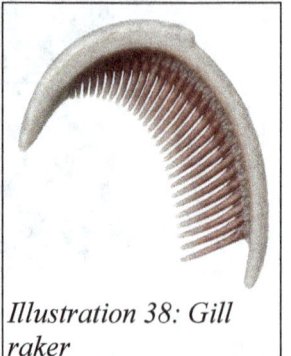
Illustration 38: Gill raker

So next time you think size equals power, remember the fangtooth: a little fish with a big bite and an even bigger secret life in the dark.

Firefly Squid: Light Show In the Sea

Imagine standing on the shore of the sea at night. The waves roll in and suddenly, the water begins to glow. Not just a faint shimmer, but a wild, blinking, flickering light show, blue lights dancing beneath the surface like an underwater rave. Welcome to Toyama Bay, Japan, where the firefly squid throws the flashiest party in the ocean every spring.

From March to June, millions of these glowing squid, *Watasenia scintillans* if you want to get scientific, gather to spawn. It's not just the ocean that gets excited. Tourists line the shore just to watch the squid's neon ballet.

The firefly squid puts on this light show using thousands of special cells called photophores, tiny spots on its skin that produce light in a deep, electric blue. These photophores are scattered all over its body, even on its twisty, grasping tentacles. The squid can light them up all at once, flash them in patterns, or blink them like nature's own Morse code. Scientists call this ability bioluminescence, but we like to call it pure sea magic.

Why all the sparkle? Well, scientists think these glowing signals help firefly squid talk to each other. They may use their lights to attract mates, like waving a glowing "hello!" in the dark. And if something tries to eat

Illustration 39: Firefly squid

them, like a hungry fish, the squid might flicker its lights in a crazy pattern to distract or confuse the predator, then make a quick getaway.

And get this. The firefly squid doesn't just glow, it sees glow. While most squid can only see in shades of gray, the firefly squid is the only known squid that can see in color. Its eyes have three kinds of light-sensing pigments, just like humans, and not one but two layers of retina in the back of its eyes. Scientists think this helps the squid tell its own lights apart from all the other glows drifting through the sea.

During the day, the firefly squid dives down to the mesopelagic zone, around 365 meters (that's about 1,200 feet) to hide from predators in the dark ocean depths. But when the sun sets, it rises into the epipelagic zone, ready to hunt.

That's right! This little squid, just 7 centimeters (or 3 inches) long, is a predator. It blinks its lights to lure small fish closer then, BAM! grabs them with its tentacles and chomps them with a sharp beak. It's like a glowing, underwater Venus flytrap only way cuter.

But the firefly squid lives fast and bright: it dies after one year. After it mates and lays its eggs, it begins to die. The eggs hatch in about a week, and a new generation of glow-squids begins its short, shining life.

In Japan, the firefly squid is more than a light show. It's also dinner. Each year, fishing boats catch about 4,500 tonnes (5,000 tons!) of them, especially during the spawning season. They're considered a delicacy, often eaten boiled or served with vinegar.

So next time you see a flashing neon sign, remember: there's a little squid out there that's been doing light shows since long before electricity. Nature always did it first and sometimes even better.

Flabby Whalefish: Transformers of the Sea

Illustration 40: Female flabby whalefish

Have you ever looked in the mirror and thought, "Yep, I definitely got Mom's eyes and Dad's nose"? That's pretty normal. Most young animals (and people) look a lot like their parents. But not the flabby whalefish (*Gyrinomimus grahami*). Not even close. In fact, if you lined up a baby, a grown-up female, and a grown-up male flabby whalefish side by side, you might think they were three completely different creatures. That's exactly what early scientists did!

This deep-sea trickery is called sexual dimorphism. Sexual dimorphism is a fancy term that means males and females look wildly different. Add in the fact that juveniles don't look like either adult males or adult females, and you've got yourself a deep-sea mystery. For a long time, scientists gave each stage its own name, believing they were separate species altogether. Only later did they realize: surprise! All three were just different life stages of the same fish.

The adult female flabby whalefish is a stretchy wonder. Her stomach is like a deep-sea balloon. It can expand to gulp down large meals whenever she finds them. That's a superpower in the dark, food-scarce bathypelagic zone, where meals are few and far between.

Now the male? He takes weird to a whole new level. When he transforms from a juvenile into an adult, his jaw fuses shut. That's right! He can't open his mouth ever again. So how does he survive? He holds onto the food he ate as a juvenile, slowly digesting it over the rest of his life. Talk about making your lunch last!

As for their name, "whalefish" comes from their oversized heads and big mouths, which kind of resemble tiny whales. But don't let the name fool you. The biggest flabby whalefish is only about 40 centimeters long (around 16 inches).

These slippery shape-shifters live way down in the bathypelagic zone, between 1.5 and 3.5 kilometers (1 to 2 miles) below the surface. That's so deep that sunlight never reaches them. But they don't mind the darkness. They're perfectly adapted to life in the deep sea.

And they're not just hiding in one part of the ocean. Flabby whalefish are found all over the world, quietly confusing scientists, gulping down rare snacks, and showing us just how bizarre and brilliant deep-sea life can be.

Frilled Shark: A Fossil With Fangs

Illustration 41: Frilled shark

Would you like to meet a living fossil that swims? Say hello to the frilled shark (*Chlamydoselachus anguineus*), a deep-sea creature so ancient-looking, it's often called a "living fossil." That's not just a fun nickname. This odd-looking shark, with its eel-like body and ruffled gill slits, has barely changed since the time of the dinosaurs! Scientists have found fossils from 95 million years ago that look almost exactly like today's frilled sharks. It's like time forgot to update this fish!

But why hasn't the frilled shark changed much in all that time? One possible answer: it never needed to. Hidden away in the shadowy depths of the mesopelagic and bathypelagic zones, between 50 and 200 meters (about 160 to 660 feet) below the surface, the frilled shark has lived in a quiet, slow-motion world where speed and flashiness aren't as important as stealth and patience.

Growing up to 2 meters long (that's about the length of a tall adult human), this shark moves with slow, snake-like grace. Its long body slithers through the water like an underwater dragon, hunting silently in the dark. It doesn't rush. It doesn't chase. It lurks. Its six pairs of frilly gills give it a ruffled, old-fashioned collar, like something out of a museum.

And then there are the teeth. Oh, the teeth! Over 300 needle-sharp teeth line its mouth in neat rows, like tiny backward-pointing hooks. Once something gets caught in there, it's not getting out. The frilled shark likes to snack on cephalopods (like squid), bony fish, and even smaller sharks. It's a creature of surprises, quiet, slow, and then suddenly, snap! Dinner is served.

As if that wasn't strange enough, the frilled shark also has one of the longest pregnancies of any animal we know. A female may carry her developing young for more than three and a half years! That's longer than an elephant's pregnancy. Scientists believe this slow reproduction is one reason why frilled sharks are so rare today. They're survivors, but not in a hurry.

The frilled shark may not win any beauty contests, but it's a master of mystery, a deep-sea time traveler, and one of nature's most astonishing throwbacks. It's like the ocean's way of keeping a secret from the past: still alive, still swimming, still utterly strange.

Giant Isopod: Giant Deep-Sea Rolly-Polly

Have you ever flipped over a rock in your backyard and found a tiny gray creature that curled into a ball? That's a rolly-polly, also called a pill bug or potato bug. Now picture one the size of your forearm, with armored plates and a face made for munching. Meet the giant isopod (*Bathynomus giganteus*), the deep sea's heavyweight crustacean and the ultimate cousin of your garden bug.

Giant isopods are an example of deep-sea gigantism. Some things in the deep ocean grow much larger than their cousins in the shallow parts of the ocean or on land. Scientists think giantism may be an adaptation to colder temperature, food scarcity, reduced predation pressure or increased dissolved oxygen concentrations in the deep sea.

These deep-sea giants scuttle along the ocean floor, in the bathyal and upper abyssal zones, usually between 365 and 730 meters (about 1,200 to 2,400 feet) deep. That's below the reach of sunlight, where the world turns cold, dark, and weird.

Illustration 42: Giant isopod

Giant isopods are the ocean's clean-up crew. They feast on anything that sinks to the seafloor, including dead fish, squid, even whale carcasses. If something is slow enough (like a sea cucumber just minding its business), the isopod might make a snack of that, too. To tackle such a buffet, it comes equipped with not one, not two, but four sets of jaws. Some jaws shred, some crush, and others slurp up whatever's left. Talk about being built for leftovers.

Because meals are few and far between in the deep sea, giant isopods have mastered the art of patience. In aquariums, some have gone eight whole weeks without a single bite. But when a feast finally arrives? They gorge until they look like they're wearing a balloon suit. They are stuffed so full they can barely move. This is because they never know when the next meal will fall from above.

Living in darkness has its challenges, but the giant isopod is well-prepared. It has compound eyes made of about 4,000 tiny lenses, perfect for detecting the faintest flicker of light. Two long pairs of antennae sweep ahead, helping it feel its way across the soft ocean floor. And with seven pairs of legs, it crawls slowly and steadily across mud or clay, usually alone, like a tank-shaped hermit.

And why are they so big? That's part of a strange rule of the deep called deep-sea gigantism. For reasons scientists still puzzle over, deep ocean animals often grow to monstrous sizes compared to their shallow-water cousins. Maybe it's the pressure, the cold, or a clever way to store energy between meals. No one knows for sure. But the result? A crustacean that can grow more than 40 centimeters (16 inches) long!

When threatened, the giant isopod does something delightfully familiar: it curls up into a tight armored ball, just like its tiny land cousins. Its seven hard, overlapping plates act like a shield, both strong and flexible. But even with all that protection, it's not invincible. Tiger sharks have been known to bite right through.

So next time you see a little rolly-polly in your garden, imagine its deep-sea cousin cruising through the twilight zone of the ocean, hungry, armored, and ready to roll.

Giant Tube Worms: The Mouthless Marvels

Illustration 43: Giant tube worms

Imagine a creature that has no mouth, no stomach, and still eats poison for a living. Say hello to the giant tube worm (*Riftia pachyptila*), one of the strangest success stories of the deep sea. These worms don't snack on plants or animals. They thrive on chemicals that would make most creatures die!

But there's a twist, they don't actually "eat" at all. Giant tube worms absorb their meals through a bright red, feathery structure on top of their heads called a plume. Think of it like a chemical straw. That plume is packed with blood vessels and turns the worm into a living chemical plant, pulling in oxygen, chemicals and a gas called hydrogen sulfide from the hot, mineral-rich water around them.

Hydrogen sulfide is a stinky gas that smells like rotten eggs. In most animals, it would shut down oxygen delivery in the blood and cause serious trouble. But the giant tube worm's blood has super-hemoglobin. Super-hemoglobin is a special version of hemoglobin that carries oxygen even in the presence of hydrogen sulfide. If humans had super-hemoglobin in our blood, we could breathe in a volcano!

Now here's where it gets even cooler. The worm itself can't digest those chemicals. So it lets bacteria do all the hard work. Inside its body is a cozy pouch filled with helpful microbes. These bacteria take the chemicals and use them as food, like tiny chefs whipping up chemical soup. The worm gets the energy it needs, and the bacteria get a place to live and their food delivered on a silver platter. Win-win!

Giant tube worms are an example of deep-sea gigantism. Some things in the deep ocean grow much larger than their cousins in the shallow parts of the ocean or on land. Scientists think giantism may be an adaptation to colder temperature, food scarcity, reduced predation pressure and increased dissolved oxygen concentrations in the deep sea.

Giant tube worms hang out near black smokers, which are deep-sea hydrothermal vents. Hydrothermal vents are cracks in the ocean floor where seawater gets superheated by magma below. The hot water gushes out, dark with dissolved minerals. Hence the name "black smoker." It's basically a deep-sea hot spring for creatures that like their water spicy and their food spicier.

But life here is risky. Black smokers don't last forever. They cool off or clog up. And the worms? They're stuck. Literally. They anchor themselves to the ocean floor and can't budge. So, when their smoker goes silent, they die. But, not before reproducing like champs.

Tube worms release clouds of egg and sperm sacs into the water. The lucky few that meet and merge become larvae, tiny floating versions of tube worms. These baby worms drift through the ocean, looking for a new black smoker to call home. When they find one, they dive down, latch onto a rock, and get to work building their tube.

Here's the trick: baby worms actually have a mouth and a gut at first. They swallow bacteria, and then *poof!* their mouth and gut vanish as they grow, trapping the bacteria inside their bodies for life. Instant food factory installed!

And they grow fast. Really fast. A giant tube worm can stretch up to 6 feet long in just a few years! When scientists discovered a brand new black smoker and came back later, they were amazed to see a whole bustling city of tube worms already set up and thriving.

Goblin Shark: Fish With an Electric Nose

Have you ever seen a creature that looks like it swam out of a dream, or maybe a nightmare? Meet the goblin shark, an eerie, ancient predator that has earned its spooky name and strange reputation. With a long, flattened

Illustration 44: Goblin shark

snout, and jaws that shoot forward like a monster from a sci-fi movie, the goblin shark (*Mitsukurina owstoni*) is one of the strangest fish in the sea.

Goblin sharks have been haunting the oceans for a very long time, about 125 million years, to be exact. That's back when dinosaurs still stomped around on land. Because goblin sharks have changed so little over millions of years, scientists call them living fossils.

Now, in fairy tales, goblins are odd little creatures with twisty features and mischievous grins. Goblin sharks don't grin at all, but their odd appearance certainly explains the name. Still, to another goblin shark, this look is probably just normal. "Nice snout you've got there," one might say to another.

Illustration 45: Fairy tale goblin

Goblin sharks are deep-sea lurkers in the sublittoral and bathyal zones. They live near the bottom of the ocean, especially along the edges of underwater continents, in places called continental slopes and shelves. They can grow up to 12 feet long and weigh around 460 pounds, though most are smaller. Because they live in such deep, dark places, humans rarely see them. Much of what we know comes from the occasional shark caught by accident or glimpsed by deep-sea submarines.

Their bodies are soft and flabby, like a jelly-filled balloon in shark form. Their fins are small. All this suggests they're not winning any swimming races. Instead, scientists think goblin sharks use the ambush method. That means they stay still and wait for an unsuspecting fish or squid to wander too close.

But how do they hunt in the pitch-black ocean where eyes are almost useless? The goblin shark has a secret weapon: its snout. That long, flat nose is packed with special organs called ampullae of Lorenzini. These help the shark sense tiny electric signals from the muscles of nearby animals. This is kind of like a built-in, electronic motion detector for living things!

And then comes the best part: the jaws. Oh, the jaws! Most sharks chomp down with jaws attached firmly to their skulls. But not the goblin shark. Its jaws are like slingshots. They're connected by stretchy tendons that pull them back toward the throat when not in use. But when prey is detected, *snap!* The jaws spring forward faster than you can blink, extending several inches in front of the face to snatch their next meal. It's like a monster movie in real life!

So if you ever meet a goblin shark, hopefully from the safety of a submarine, remember: you're looking at one of the ocean's oldest, weirdest wonders. Part shark. Part throwback. Part nightmare. All awesome.

Gummy Squirrel: Sea Cucumber That Looks Like Candy

Imagine a creature that looks a little like a squishy gummy candy and a little like a squirrel with a tail fluttering behind it. Now, put that creature at the bottom of the ocean, and you've got the delightfully odd gummy squirrel (*Psychropotes longicauda*)!

Despite the name, this creature is not made of sugar, and it definitely doesn't scamper through trees. The gummy squirrel is actually a kind of sea cucumber, a squishy invertebrate that belongs to a group of animals more closely related to sea stars than squirrels. It lives far below the ocean's surface in one of the deepest, darkest places on Earth, the abyssal plain.

Illustration 46: Gummy squirrel

Adult gummy squirrels crawl along the seafloor using tube feet. These are tiny suction-like limbs that help them move slowly across the ooze. Around their mouths, they have a circle of feeding tentacles that scoop up sediment. It's not the mud they want, they want the microscopic bits of food in the mud. They sift through it like picky eaters at a buffet, selecting tasty morsels of decaying plants and animals that have drifted down from above.

But here's where things get extra strange. The larvae of the gummy squirrel live in the open ocean, floating in the pelagic zone. This means that young gummy squirrels live high above the ocean floor, drifting through the water like microscopic astronauts. Unlike most larvae that feed as they grow, gummy squirrel larvae don't seem to eat anything at all. Scientists believe they survive entirely off the yolk stored in their oversized eggs. This is like packing a lunch big enough to last for the entire first stage of life!

And what about that "squirrel tail"? That's one of the most distinctive parts of this creature. The long, flat, and sometimes ruffled tail is thought to help them glide gently through the water, although some scientists think it might just be for show. In a world of darkness, anything that stands out is fascinating.

Though rarely seen, the gummy squirrel has become something of a fan favorite in deep-sea biology. It's soft, strange, and so very mysterious. Just one more reason the deep ocean is like nature's alien world, waiting to be explored.

Helmet Jellyfish: Glowing Red Helmet

Imagine a creature from the deep that wears a glowing red helmet and drifts silently through the blackness like a ghost from a sci-fi movie. Meet the helmet jellyfish (*Periphylla periphylla*), one of the strangest and most mysterious jellyfish in the ocean.

This deep-sea drifter gets its name from the shape of its bell. The bell is smooth, pointed, and dome-like, it really does look like a

Illustration 47: Helmet jellyfish

helmet from a knight's suit of armor. But instead of charging into battle, the helmet jellyfish floats in eerie silence through the inky depths of the sea, flashing red light as it goes.

Yes! Flashing red lights! The helmet jellyfish is bioluminescent, which means it can create its own light using chemical reactions in its body. Unlike many deep-sea animals that glow blue, this jellyfish produces deep red flashes, like a warning light pulsing in the darkness. Scientists believe these red flashes may be a way for jellyfish to communicate with each other, but we still don't know exactly what they're saying. Maybe it's jellyfish Morse code.

Helmet jellyfish are nearly invisible to the naked eye at depth because they are made almost entirely of water, a whopping 90%! The rest is made up of soft, jelly-like tissue. They can grow up to 30 centimeters (12 inches) long and have exactly twelve graceful tentacles that trail behind them like ribbons in the dark.

Here's where it gets even weirder: the jellyfish's skin can sense light. It contains a special pigment that reacts to brightness, but in a dangerous way. Too much light makes the pigment toxic, so helmet jellyfish are like extreme introverts, they avoid light at all costs. That's why they stick to the deep ocean, the mesopelagic and bathypelagic zones, where it's cold, dark, and safe from sunshine. They prefer chilly waters between 4° and 11° Celsius (39° to 52° Fahrenheit), and are found all over the world except the Arctic Ocean, which is just a little too extreme even for them.

By day, helmet jellyfish dive to incredible depths, sometimes as deep as 7,000 meters (23,000 feet) in the abyssopelagic and hadalpelagic zones! They perform a nightly commute called vertical migration, slowly rising toward the surface to snack on zooplankton (tiny floating animals). At dawn, they descend again into the abyss, like silent red lanterns sinking into the gloom. If the ocean surface is stirred up by strong winds, these jellyfish wisely skip the surface trip and stay deep, avoiding the rough ride.

They also have an incredible ability to survive in low-oxygen waters, something not many animals can handle. Inside their gelatinous bodies are chemicals that help them thrive in the deep, where oxygen is scarce.

Now here's a final twist: when a helmet jellyfish has babies, it doesn't hatch into a larva like most jellyfish. Instead, it hatches into a tiny jellyfish that looks just like a miniature adult. It's like being born ready to go! This is possible because their eggs are packed with an extra-large yolk, a sort of deep-sea lunchbox that gives the baby all the energy it needs to grow before it ever starts feeding.

In some parts of the world, like the Norwegian fjords, helmet jellyfish are becoming so common that they've started to compete with fish for food, which causes trouble for the local fishing industry. But even when they cause problems, there's no denying these otherworldly creatures are some of the ocean's most enchanting enigmas.

Japanese Spider Crab: The Gentle Giant with Sticky Style

Meet the ocean's lankiest leggy beast, the Japanese spider crab (*Macrocheira kaempferi*). This enormous crustacean holds the record for

Illustration 48: Japanese spider crab

the longest leg span of any arthropod (that's the animal club that includes bugs, spiders, and crabs). From claw tip to claw tip, its legs can stretch a whopping 3.7 meters (over 12 feet), that's longer than some cars!

These crabs are true deep-sea dwellers, hanging out in the chilly waters of the bathyal zone around southern Japan, usually between 50 and 600 meters deep (160 and 2,000 feet). Imagine tiptoeing across the ocean floor in near-darkness for over a hundred years. Because yes, these creatures can live that long!

To stay safe from predators, the Japanese spider crab wears armor, a hard, bumpy exoskeleton that acts like both a shield and a disguise. But they don't stop there. These sneaky decorators pick up sponges, seaweed, and even sea critters, sticking them on their backs like fashion accessories. Their motto? "If it helps me blend in, it's going on my shell!"

Though they look fierce, these crabs are not picky eaters. They're omnivores, which means they munch on both plants and animals. Dead fish? Sure. A tasty mollusk? Yum. With powerful claws strong enough to pry open shells, they tear their food into bite-sized bits before gobbling it up. Since they can't swim, they scuttle across the seafloor, always on the hunt for their next snack.

And when it comes to babies, these crabs don't mess around. A single female can carry up to 1.5 million eggs under her belly in a single year! After about 10 days, the eggs hatch into tiny larvae that float up to the ocean's surface like miniature explorers, feeding and growing before they make their way back down to the deep.

But not all is well in crab country. The Japanese spider crab has become a popular seafood delicacy, and overfishing has taken its toll. In 1976, about 24.7 tonnes of these crabs were caught. Less than a decade later, that number dropped to just 3.2 tonnes. That's like going from a full buffet to a single shrimp cocktail.

To help these leggy wonders make a comeback, people in Japan are raising crab eggs in safe environments and releasing the young crabs back into the wild. It's a race against time, but with a little help, maybe these gentle giants will keep creeping across the ocean floor for centuries to come.

Lanternfish: Tiny Swimmers, Big Light Show

Illustration 49: Lanternfish

If the ocean held a popularity contest, the lanternfish might just win by sheer numbers! These deep-sea dynamos from the family *Myctophidae* are everywhere. Seriously! If you added up the weight of all the lanternfish in the world, it would be more than half the weight of all the fish in the entire ocean. That's a whole lot of glowing fish!

Why "lanternfish"? Because they glow like little swimming nightlights. Along their sides, they have photophores, special organs that produce light. These can shine in hues of blue, green, or yellow, and some lanternfish even sport lights under their eyes or on their bellies. Scientists believe lanternfish use these twinkling lights for counterillumination. They match the dim light filtering down from above, making them invisible to predators lurking below. Sneaky, right?

Now here's a sonar story with a twist. When the Navy first used sonar, like radar, but with sound instead of radio waves, they spotted something odd: a "false bottom" in the ocean. At first, they thought it was a mistake. But it wasn't the ocean floor at all. It was a massive swarm of lanternfish, floating so densely that the sonar bounced off them as if they were land! The culprit? Their swim bladders, air-filled sacs that help the fish rise and sink. Sound waves bounce off those bladders just like they bounce off the seafloor.

Even though lanternfish are small (most are only 2 to 30 centimeters long, less than a foot), they pull off an epic daily commute. During the day, they dive down into the dark bathypelagic zone. That's 300 to 1,500 meters (980 to 4,920 feet) deep, where it's pitch black and the pressure is intense. But when night falls, they migrate upward to feed near the surface. This up-and-down journey is called vertical migration, and it's the largest migration by number of animals on the planet!

Why go to all that trouble? Food, of course! Lanternfish love munching on zooplankton, which also make their own nightly journey toward the surface. So up the lanternfish go, swimming silently in the moonlit depths, glowing gently as they hunt.

Tiny, glowing, mysterious and maybe the most important fish you've never seen. That's the lanternfish.

Long Nosed Chimaera: Jet-Nosed Ghost of the Deep

Illustration 50: Long nosed chimaera

What would you think if a ghostly fish with a long, pointy nose glided past you in the deep, dark ocean? Would you think it was part submarine, part stingray, part… something else? Meet the long-nosed chimaera (family *Rhinochimaeridae*), a creature so strange it seems like it was dreamed up in a science fiction movie. Chimaera is pronounced ky-MEER-uh.

Its nose is long and thin, shaped like the nose of a supersonic jet. But this nose isn't just for looks. It helps the chimaera sense tiny movements and electric fields in the water, sort of like a built-in radar system. Scientists believe that both jet planes and long-nosed chimaeras have pointy noses for the same reason: to slice smoothly through their surroundings, air for planes, water for the chimaera.

The word "chimaera" comes from ancient Greek mythology. A chimera was a fire-breathing monster made of parts from different animals, a lion, a goat, and a snake, all rolled into one. The long-nosed chimaera doesn't breathe fire (thank goodness), but it does look like a mash-up of animals. It has a long snout like a swordfish, a body like a shark, and big flapping fins like wings. No wonder it's sometimes called the Pacific spookfish.

Illustration 51: Mythological Chimaera

And here's a spooky surprise. On its back, right behind the head, is a sharp spine rising out of the dorsal fin. This isn't just for show, it's venomous, like the fang of a rattlesnake or the stinger of a wasp. But don't worry! The long-nosed chimaera lives in the deep sea in the bathyal zone, between 330 and 1,490 meters down (that's 1,060 to 4,900 feet) near the ocean floor. That's much deeper than most people ever swim, dive, or even send submarines.

With its haunting look, deep-dwelling lifestyle, and electric-sensing snout, the long-nosed chimaera is one of the ocean's most mysterious and magical monsters. If you ever see one in person, you're either very lucky, or very, very deep.

Mariana Snailfish: Champion of the Abyss

Illustration 52: Mariana snailfish

How low can you go? A few feet under water in a pool? Maybe a few meters with scuba gear? Well, get ready to meet a fish that leaves all of us in the shallow end. The Mariana snailfish (*Pseudoliparis swirei*) holds the title for deepest known fish on Earth, swimming calmly through the crushing darkness of the hadal zone nearly eight and a half kilometers below the surface. That's over 27,000 feet, or about five miles deep!

This champion of the abyss lives in the Mariana Trench, the deepest part of the world's oceans. The trench itself is a giant scar in the Earth's crust, stretching about 2,550 kilometers (1,500 miles) long and plunging to a depth of 11 kilometers (almost 7 miles) at its deepest point. That's deeper than Mount Everest is tall!

But the Mariana snailfish isn't flashy. In fact, it's pinkish and partly see-through, like a ghost made of jelly. Why bother with camouflage when there's no light down there? It's a world of pitch-black silence, and the snailfish has adapted beautifully to it. It grows to about 28.8 centimeters (11.3 inches), just under a foot long, and weighs around 160 grams (about a third of a pound). That's lighter than a can of soup!

What does it eat down there, where almost nothing lives? Tiny shrimp-like creatures called crustaceans. The snailfish simply slurps them up with its mouth which is adapted to the pressure of the deep. Speaking of pressure, down where it lives, the pressure is 350 times greater than at sea level. Imagine 350 elephants standing on your head! That's the kind of squeeze we're talking about! But the Mariana snailfish doesn't mind. In fact, if you brought one up to the surface, it would puff up and fall apart. Its body is specially built for deep living.

Here's something even more amazing. Scientists believe that baby Mariana snailfish, called larvae, might start their lives in much shallower water. Once they've grown enough, they migrate down into the crushing dark. It's like starting life on a sunny beach and then slowly moving to live on the bottom of a black, ice-cold canyon.

The Mariana snailfish lives in the hadalpelagic zone, a part of the ocean so deep, its name comes from Hades, the Greek god of the underworld. It's a place with no sunlight, no plants, and barely any sound. And yet, life finds a way. Delicate, strange, and surprisingly graceful, the Mariana snailfish is a soft-bodied reminder that even the darkest corners of our planet are full of wonder.

Marine Hatchetfish: Shadow Snatcher

Imagine your eyes suddenly turned into telescopes, pointing straight up, helping you spot snacks floating above. That's what life is like for the marine hatchetfish! With eyes shaped like tubes that aim toward the ocean's ceiling, these deep-sea hunters can see the faintest flickers of light, even in the twilight world far below the surface in the mesopelagic zone.

By day, the marine hatchetfish (family *Sternoptychidae*) hides in the gloom of the deep. But at night, it drifts upwards, near the shallows, and becomes a shadow stalker. Picture this: a fish is swimming above, barely blocking the dim glow from the surface. The hatchetfish is lurking just below. It spots the shadow, angles its body upward, and snap! its upturned mouth opens wide and swallows dinner.

But hunting shadows has its risks. What's to stop another predator from spotting its shadow and making a meal of the hatchetfish? That's where one of the coolest tricks in the deep sea comes in, counterillumination! The marine hatchetfish has a glowing belly. Yes, a

Illustration 53: Marine hatchetfish

belly that shines! Tiny organs called photophores produce light through a chemical reaction (like a firefly's twinkle). This belly-glow is carefully tuned to match the light from above, so when a predator looks up, the hatchetfish's outline disappears. It's like an invisibility cloak made of light!

And that's not its only disguise. The marine hatchetfish is incredibly thin, almost like it's been squished sideways. So when it is seen from below, it's barely there. Combine this flatness with belly-light magic, and you've got a fish that's almost impossible to spot.

There are about forty-five species of marine hatchetfish, each with its own sparkle and strategy. You can find them cruising the deep in tropical and subtropical waters of the Atlantic, Pacific, and Indian Oceans, usually between 250 and 600 meters deep (that's like stacking 3 Empire State Buildings on top of each other underwater!). But sometimes they dive down as deep as 1,370 meters or swim up as high as 180 meters. It's a daily vertical commute!

They may be tiny, ranging from 2.8 centimeters (just about the length of your thumb) to 12 centimeters (about the width of your hand), but marine hatchetfish pack a lot of wonder into their silvery frames.

As for baby hatchetfish? Scientists are still piecing that mystery together. They know hatchetfish don't babysit. Once the eggs are released, they're on their own. And they believe that marine hatchetfish live fast and glow bright, usually for just one year. Short life, deep dives, and some of the best camouflage in the ocean? Not bad for a fish that can vanish in plain sight.

Megamouth Shark: Eats Like a Whale

Illustration 54: Megamouth shark

When you hear the word shark, you probably picture something fierce and fast, perhaps an ocean predator packed with teeth, slicing its dinner into bite-sized chunks. But not all sharks are built for chomping! Meet the megamouth shark (*Megachasma pelagios*) a gentle giant with a dinner plate for a mouth and a diet that's more like a whale's than a warrior's.

The first megamouth ever found made quite the splash, literally! In 1976, it got tangled in the sea anchor of a Navy ship off the coast of Hawai'i. Before that, no one even knew this shark existed. By 2018, fewer than 100 had been seen or captured. That makes it one of the rarest sharks known to science, like the deep sea's secret superhero.

Megamouths are deep divers. They prefer the mysterious **mesopelagic** zone of the ocean, cruising between 150 to 1,000 meters (that's up to 3,280 feet deep!). They're found in warm and mild oceans all around the globe, but you'll need some serious scuba skills and probably a submarine to spot one.

Now here's the jaw-dropping part. The megamouth's mouth can be over 1.2 meters (4 feet) wide, as wide as a second grader is tall! But don't worry, it's not looking to bite you. Instead of hunting like most sharks, this one just opens wide and swims forward. It's called a ram feeder. Like a slow-moving vacuum cleaner, it slurps up plankton and jellyfish, tiny creatures floating in the sea.

Inside that gaping mouth are gill rakers, comb like filters that catch the snacks and let the water flow out. Anything big enough to get trapped gets swallowed. Anything smaller floats on by, totally safe. That's why the megamouth has teeny tiny teeth: it doesn't need to bite, just filter and feast.

Plankton have a habit of rising toward the surface at night and sinking back down during the day, a dance called vertical migration. And guess what? The megamouth follows them, riding the ocean elevator up and down each day, slowly gliding with its glowing smile.

Wait. Glowing? That's right! The megamouth has a shiny white band around its lips, and scientists believe it might glow in the dark using photophores, tiny light-making organs. It's like a neon sign flashing "Buffet for plankton this way!"

These sharks can grow to 18 feet long and weigh more than a small car, over 1180 kilograms (2,600 pounds!). But even though they're huge, they move at a leisurely pace, drifting through the deep with all the chill of a giant sea cloud.

And how are baby megamouths born? The mother carries the fertilized eggs inside her body until they hatch. Then the baby sharks eat unfertilized eggs. That's kind of like a breakfast buffet before they're born. Once they're ready, out they swim, fully formed and ready to face the world on their own.

In the world of deep sea monsters, the megamouth shark is a shy and slow-moving mystery, a real-life sea dragon that prefers soup to steak, and glows like a lantern in the dark.

Oarfish: Sea Serpent of the Deep

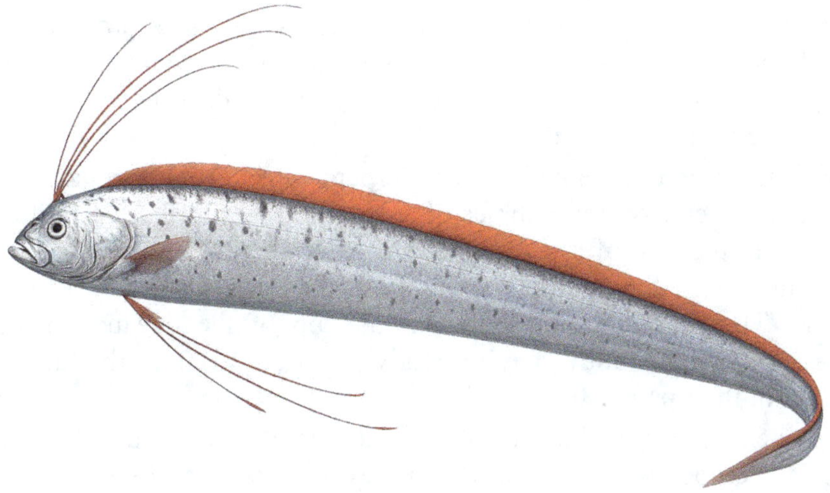

Illustration 55: Oarfish

Once upon a wave, in the days of wooden ships and salty legends, sailors spun stories of sea serpents, monsters as long as ships, with glittering scales and eyes like moons. But what if those sea serpents weren't just tall tales? What if they were real… and just really misunderstood?

Enter the oarfish (family *Regalecidae*), the true sea serpents of the deep. With its ribbon-like body, shimmery silver scales, and bright red crest-like fins, the oarfish looks like something from a myth. It's no wonder ancient mariners thought they'd spotted something supernatural. The oarfish is the longest bony fish known to science, stretching up to 17 meters (that's 56 feet, longer than a school bus!). And it's no featherweight either, tipping the scales at 272 kilograms (around 600 pounds).

In Japan it's known as the "Messenger from the Sea God's Palace." Sounds magical, right? And maybe there's some mystery to that name. Japanese folklore says that oarfish appear before big earthquakes. Between December 2009 and March 2010, several oarfish washed ashore in Japan. Then, in March 2011, a massive earthquake struck. Could the oarfish be nature's early warning system? Scientists aren't sure. There just isn't enough evidence yet. But the idea has definitely sparked curiosity.

Normally, oarfish live deep down in the mesopelagic zone, about 200 meters (650 feet) beneath the waves, though they've been spotted as deep as 1,000 meters (3,300 feet). That's well into the twilight zone of the ocean. But when they're sick or near the end of their lives, they sometimes rise to the surface. That's when people get a rare chance to see these ghostly creatures up close.

Unlike most fish that swish their tails to swim, the oarfish has a different groove. It ripples its long dorsal fin like a wave, propelling itself through the water in a hypnotic dance. Some scientists even believe it might have the power to zap with electricity, perhaps to daze its prey or spook predators. Shocking, isn't it?

When it's time to make baby sea serpents, the oarfish lets its eggs drift up to the surface like tiny bubbles of color. Each egg is about 6 millimeters wide (about the size of a pencil eraser). After about three weeks, the eggs hatch into larvae, miniature versions of the long fish they'll someday become. These youngsters float near the top of the ocean, feasting on microscopic meals until they're ready to descend into the deep blue shadows of their parents.

So next time you hear a tale of sea serpents slithering through the waves, remember, sometimes the truth is even more marvelous than myth.

Pompeii worm: The Hottest Home on Earth

How hot is too hot? Most people start sweating when it hits 30°C (86°F). A long soak in a 45°C (113°F) hot tub would send you scrambling for cold water and lemonade. Now imagine living in water heated up to 105°C (221°F), hotter than boiling! For us, that would be like living in a lava Jacuzzi. But for the Pompeii worm (*Alvinella pompejana*), that's just another day at the office.

Illustration 56: Pompeii worm out of its tube

These squiggly survivors make their homes on the scalding chimneys of black smokers, deep under the sea. Black smokers are underwater vents that spew out superheated, mineral-rich water from beneath Earth's crust. It's dark. It's deadly hot. It's packed with toxic chemicals. And the Pompeii worm loves it.

Despite the wild heat, these worms manage to keep their bodies a cool 20-30°C (68-86°F). How? Scientists are still piecing the puzzle together, but they have some pretty fascinating ideas.

One theory is that the worms act like tiny living radiators. They may send extra heat away from their bodies and toward their gills, which stick out into cooler water. There, the gills can dump heat into the sea, like little heat vents.

But there's more. Take a look at a Pompeii worm's back. It's fuzzy! But that's not hair. That's a living coat of bacteria. These bacteria form thick, woolly colonies on the worm's back, and scientists think they're doing more than just hitching a ride. Some believe the bacteria might be producing heat-shielding proteins, turning the worm's back into a microbial fireproof jacket!

This symbiosis may go both ways. The worm offers the bacteria a cozy place to live, right next to the nutrient-rich vent water. In return, the bacteria might protect the worm from both heat and toxic chemicals. It's a win-win in the most extreme neighborhood on Earth.

Hungry? So is the Pompeii worm. But there aren't any pizzas or plankton down here. Instead, it dines on chemosynthetic bacteria, microscopic life forms that eat the chemicals gushing out of black smokers. As the water flows by, the worms filter out bacteria to eat. They are called filter feeders. So, the worm munches on bacteria that eat poison. Talk about a strange food chain!

These worms can grow up to 13 centimeters (about 5 inches) about the length of a hot dog. Not bad for a creature living in what's basically a volcanic vent.

One last twist. Baby Pompeii worms can't survive where the adults live. It's simply too extreme. So scientists think the worms lay their eggs in cooler water. The eggs drift, hatch, and the tiny wormlets find their way to a smoker vent and settle down. Welcome to the hottest real estate in the ocean!

Sea Angel: Winged Wonder

What kind of angel flaps through icy waters instead of fluffy clouds? Meet the sea angel (*Clione limacina*) a ghostly, winged wonder that drifts and dances through the dark blue of the deep. It's not really an angel (and definitely not a bug!), but a shell-less sea slug with wing-like fins that flap as it swims, earning it the nickname "naked sea butterfly." Sounds magical, right?

Sea angels glide through the cold, clear waters of the Arctic and North Atlantic Oceans, anywhere from the surface down to 500 meters (that's about a third of a mile deep!). They live in the upper layers of the ocean, called the epipelagic and mesopelagic zones where light starts to fade and mysteries begin to glow.

Illustration 57: Sea angel

There are two known types: a northern subspecies that can grow up to 8.5 centimeters (3.3 inches) and a southern one that tops out at around 3 centimeters (1.2 inches). Other than size, they look nearly the same: sleek, transparent, and just a little spooky.

But don't let their angelic name fool you. These fluttering floaters are fearsome hunters. Their favorite meal? The sea butterfly (*Limacina*), a tiny sea snail with a delicate shell. Here's how it works:

First, the sea angel uses six tentacle-like arms called buccal cones to grab its prey. Then, it twists the poor sea butterfly until its shell's opening faces forward. Next, out come two clusters of tiny hooks that reach inside, latch onto the snail's soft body, and yank it out. Shell? Tossed. Slug? Swallowed. Ouch.

And guess what? Sea angels can even eat other sea angels, especially when snacks are scarce. But they can also go up to a year without food. Talk about patience! When times are really tough, they might nibble on amphipods and calanoids, tiny sea critters that drift through the ocean like living sprinkles.

Despite being hunters, sea angels don't sit at the top of the food chain. They're a favorite snack for filter-feeders, like whales, who scoop them up along with other morsels.

And like many deep-sea oddballs, sea angels don't fit neatly into boy or girl categories. They're hermaphrodites, meaning each one has both sperm and eggs. When two sea angels fall for each other (or just bump into each other mid-swim), they fertilize each other's eggs. They both lay about 30-40 eggs. Their babies hatch with shells but ditch them as they grow, trading armor for freedom.

So the next time you imagine an angel, picture one with see-through skin, flapping wings, a hunger for snails, and a home deep beneath the waves.

Sea Pig: Party Animal of the Deep

Imagine living so deep in the ocean that it's always dark and your best buddy is a crab! Meet the sea pig, one of the strangest and squishiest creatures you'll never find in a petting zoo. This odd little animal (its scientific name is *Scotoplanes globosa*) often has a crab pal tagging along, usually

Illustration 58: Sea pig

a red-legged lithodid crab. Scientists don't know exactly why these two hang out together, but they do it so often that scientists think they might be helping each other in some mysterious way. That kind of friendship is called a symbiotic relationship, a relationship where each helps the other..

The sea pig was first discovered over 100 years ago by a Swedish scientist named Hjalmar Théel during an ocean adventure aboard the HMS Challenger. They were searching the deep sea for creatures nobody had ever seen before, and the sea pig was one of them!

Sea pigs are total party animals. Not the loud, dance-around kind, but the kind that loves being with friends. You'll often see them in groups of 10 to 30. Sometimes even more than 600 gather together! A group of sea pigs is called a trawl. That's a pretty fun word, don't you think?

But not everyone in the sea is friendly. Some tiny troublemakers, like parasitic snails and crustaceans, bore little holes into sea pigs' skin to snack on them. Poor sea pigs!

Sea pigs are soft and squishy with a pale, translucent (see-through) white color. They're small, only about 2 to 5 centimeters long (that's the size of a walnut!). They have lots of legs that look like tiny tubes, including some sticking out of their backs. Scientists aren't quite sure what the top legs are for. Maybe they help the sea pig sniff out snacks.

These little piggies live on abyssal plains, which are flat, wide parts of the seafloor, about 1,000 meters (3,300 feet) deep. That's more than half a mile underwater! They've even been spotted in the deepest parts of the ocean.

And what do sea pigs eat? Pretty much anything that falls from above! That includes dead animals and something called marine snow, tiny bits of plants, poop, and other drifting sea bits. They use sticky, gooey tentacles to grab the food and lift it to their mouths. It's like having spaghetti arms covered in glue, perfect for scooping up underwater leftovers! Some sea pigs even gather around giant whale carcasses to feast together like it's a deep-sea buffet.

So next time you think of pigs, don't forget the deep-sea version: the sea pig! Squishy, strange, and living life on the ocean floor.

Sea Toad: Lure-Master of the Deep

When is a toad not a toad? When it's a sea toad, of course! Sea toads (family *Chaunacidae*) don't croak, hop, or lounge on lily pads. They don't live in ponds or climb trees. They live in the deep sea, the bathyal zone, so deep that sunlight never reaches their mysterious world.

Illustration 59: Sea toad

Now, imagine a squishy little football with fins instead of legs, and a pouty face that looks like it's always slightly annoyed. That's your sea toad! With its round body, stubby tail, and flippery pelvic fins that look a lot like tiny feet, the sea toad is one of the ocean's oddest bottom-dwellers.

But those "feet" aren't just for show. Sea toads use them to sit up on the seafloor like they're resting in a comfy underwater chair. And when they're feeling adventurous (which isn't often), they use those same fins to push off and swim, gliding clumsily through the water like a grumpy little balloon with wings.

Sea toads are masters of patience. They don't chase their food. They wait for it. Perched on the ocean floor, barely moving, they use a sneaky trick to attract their next meal. Right on top of their heads is a special fin that ends in a glowing, wiggly knob. This bioluminescent lure works just like a fishing lure. Except, the sea toad is the fisherman, and the fish? They're dinner.

That little glowing ball bobs and sways in front of the sea toad's mouth, pretending to be a tasty treat. A curious fish sees the light, swims in for a closer look and SNAP! The sea toad's mouth, which opens up and down like a trapdoor instead of side to side, sucks the fish in before it even knows what hit it.

But how does the sea toad know when prey is near? It has an amazing superpower: the lateral line. This is a special organ that runs along each side of its body, letting it feel tiny movements and vibrations in the water. It's like having a built-in motion detector. If a shrimp twitches or a fish flutters by, the sea toad can sense it without even opening its eyes.

And here's where the sea toad gets extra sneaky. When it breathes, it doesn't do quick in-and-out puffs like we do. Instead, it inhales a big gulp of water into a stretchy gill sack and holds it for up to four whole minutes! During that time, the sea toad barely moves a muscle. It becomes a statue, perfectly still, almost invisible to predators and prey. This breath-holding trick also quiets the water around it, making it easier to detect tiny movements from other sea creatures.

Sea toads aren't picky eaters. If something swims by, and it fits in their mouth, they'll try to eat it. Worms, fish, tiny crustaceans, anything goes. They're like the vacuum cleaners of the deep, sucking up anything that wanders too close to their glowing lure.

So while the sea toad might not win any beauty contests, don't be fooled. It's a patient hunter, a clever ambusher, and a deep-sea expert in the art of surprise. In the darkest parts of the ocean, where strange is normal, the sea toad sits, silent, still, and ready to devour.

Sea Toad: Lure-Master of the Deep

Siphonophore: The Colony That Pretends to Be One Animal

Imagine you're swimming in the deep, dark ocean and you spot something long and glowing, like a living rope made of jelly. It moves with quiet grace, drifting through the water like a ghostly parade. Is it a single animal? Not really. It's a siphonophore (order *Siphonophore*), an animal made of many animals working together like a floating city!

When most animals grow, their cells become different parts of their bodies like lungs, legs, and eyes. But siphonophores don't just grow different parts. They grow different creatures! Each little part of a siphonophore is a full animal on its own, called a zooid. And here's the wild part: none of them can survive alone. But together, they become something incredible.

You can think of a siphonophore like a spaceship crew. Each zooid has its job:

The Eaters — These are the gastrozooids, the chefs of the colony. They have long stinging tentacles, like jellyfish, and they're in charge of catching plankton, which are tiny floating plants and animals. Once they catch the food, they digest it, then share it with the whole colony. Talk about teamwork!

The Swimmers — These are the nectophores, little jet engines that help the colony move through the ocean. They puff out water in tiny bursts, and together they push the whole siphonophore forward. The group of swimmers is called the nectosome. When they work together, it's like a squad of oars moving a boat.

The Floaters — Meet the pneumatophores, the flotation experts. These zooids are like built-in balloons, full of gas. If the siphonophore wants to float up, they inflate. If it needs to sink, they deflate. It's like having your very own hot-air balloon built right into your body!

The Growers — Baby zooids come from tiny buds, like flowers on a stem. These buds grow out from other zooids. Sometimes, a whole branch of zooids breaks off and floats away, starting a brand-new colony.

Now, if you're thinking, "Wait, does that mean a siphonophore is more like a coral reef than a jellyfish?" You're on the right track! But it's also not like a coral, because it moves through the ocean and has parts that help it swim, hunt, and float. It's part creature, part team, part living machine.

And just like there are many types of jellyfish or fish, there are many types of siphonophores. Some are just a few inches long. Others can be over 30 meters (100 feet) long. that's longer than a blue whale, the biggest animal on Earth! Some glow in the dark, lighting up the deep sea like a twinkling ribbon.

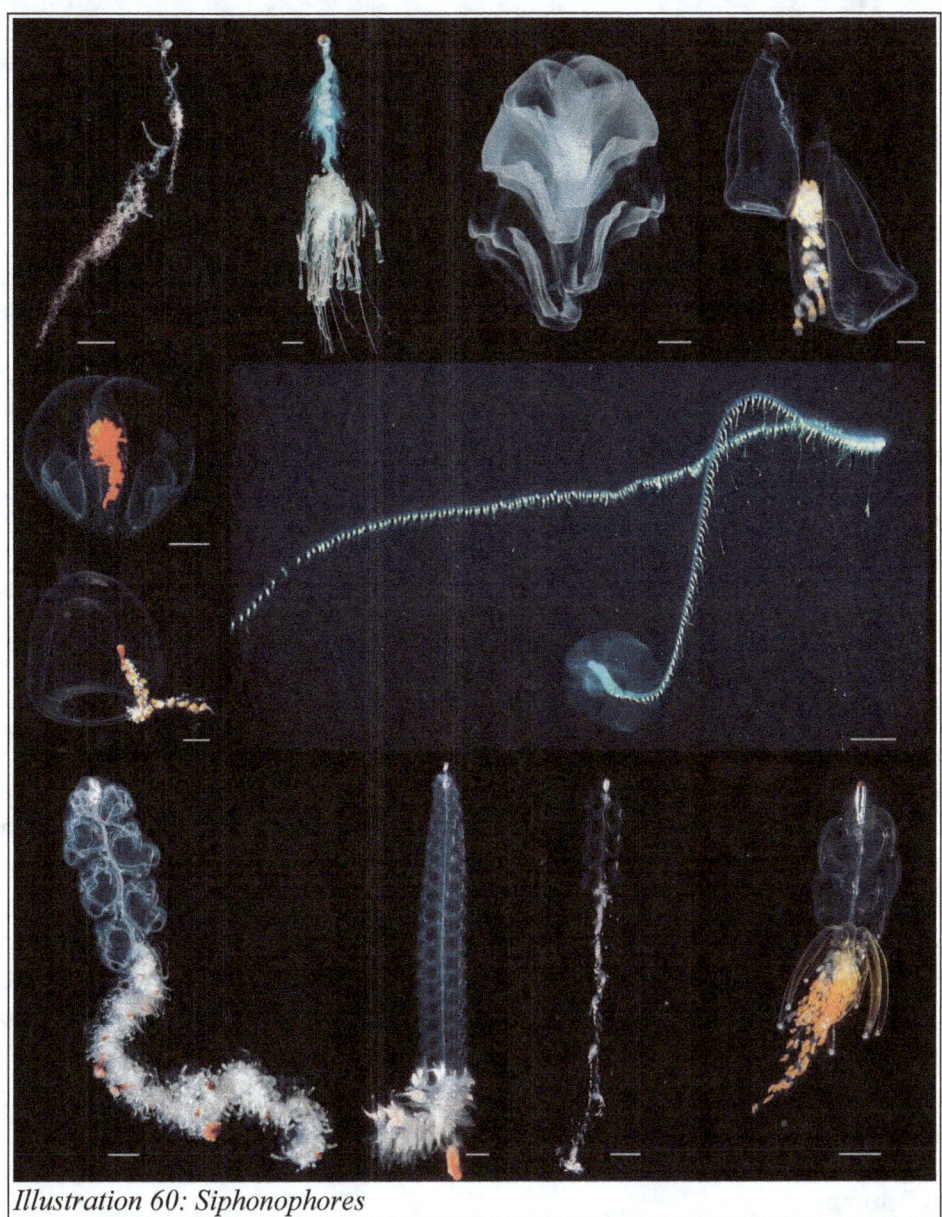

Illustration 60: Siphonophores

Siphonophores can be found all over the ocean, from the sunny surface (called the epipelagic zone) to the cold, crushing darkness of the hadalpelagic zone, which is deeper than the height of Mount Everest turned upside down!

So the next time you imagine a sea creature, picture this: a glowing, drifting wonder made up of dozens or even hundreds of little animals, all playing their part, all sticking together, all making one shimmering, floating being. That's a siphonophore. One of the most unusual and magical animals in the sea.

Slender Snipe Eel: Duck Beak on a String

When is a duck not a duck? When it's five feet long, shaped like a spaghetti noodle, and lives where sunlight never dares to dive! Meet the slender snipe eel (*Nemichthys scolopaceus*) sometimes nicknamed the "deep sea duck" because its beak-like mouth looks like it should quack instead of snap.

But don't let that silly name fool you. This eel is a marvel of the deep. It's super skinny. So skinny, in fact, that even at 1.5 meters (5 feet) long (almost as long as your bed!), it weighs less than a bottle of soda. Think of a living shoelace with eyes and a hook-toothed grin.

What's even weirder? The slender snipe eel is 75 times longer

Illustration 61: Slender snipe eel

than it is wide. If you were that long compared to your width, you'd be as tall as a four-story building! And inside that long, bendy body? A whopping 750 backbones! Humans only get 33. This eel is practically a vertebrae factory.

Now let's talk about that wacky mouth. Its jaws curve outward and never actually close. Each jaw is lined with tiny, backward-facing hooks, perfect for snatching shrimp-like snacks as the eel swishes its beak side to side through the water. Hook, snag, slurp. Yum!

And those eyes? Huge! Because where the slender snipe eel lives in the bathypelagic zone, 100 to 1,000 meters (325 to over 3,000 feet) deep. It's always in the twilight zone. Having big eyes is a must for spotting meals in the gloom.

Slender snipe eels are deep-sea mystery machines. Scientists know little about how they reproduce because they're so hard to study. But here's what they think: males grow giant nostrils as they get older. This is possibly to sniff out females in the dark. Once they mate, both parents die. The female's eggs float to the surface and hatch into larvae shaped like translucent (see-through) leaves. These ghostly leaf-larvae eventually drift down into the dark and transform into the long, twisty adults.

So next time you're thinking about ducks, remember: not all beaks go "quack." Some go fishing in the deep!

Sperm Whale: Deep Diving Mammal

Illustration 62: Sperm whale

Imagine holding your breath, diving into the ocean, and swimming down, down, down, so deep that sunlight disappears and the pressure could crush a submarine. That's just a regular afternoon for the sperm whale (*Physeter macrocephalus*).

Even though they're ocean giants, sperm whales are mammals like us. That means they need air to breathe. Since they must breath air they generally live in the epipelagic zone at the surface. To eat, they will dive into the deep black of the bathypelagic zone as far as 2,250 meters (7,382 feet)! That's deeper than the tallest mountain in the Rockies is high. They are the second deepest diving mammal, with Cuvier's beaked whale (*Ziphius cavirostris*) the very deepest.

Now here's a cool fact: if you or I tried diving that deep, our ribs would likely snap under the pressure. Ouch. But not the sperm whale! Their ribs are attached to the spine with thick, bendy cartilage. Instead of breaking, their rib cages flex like a champion yoga master.

What are they diving for? Dinner, of course. They eat mostly squid, including the legendary giant squid! Although sperm whales have teeth, they don't bother chewing. Instead, they gulp their prey whole. Inside their massive bodies is a four-chambered stomach. The first chamber grinds up the squid with powerful muscles, kind of like having an inner blender. The next three chambers handle digestion. Fancy, huh?

There's just one problem: squid beaks. Hard, indigestible, and kind of creepy, these beaks don't break down in the whale's stomach. So, what do sperm whales do? They vomit most of them up! (Gross, but efficient.) Some beaks make it all the way through and get pooped out instead. Either way, the beaks don't stick around.

Let's talk brains, because the sperm whale has the largest brain on Earth. It can weigh up to nine kilograms (20 pounds)! That's more than six times the weight of a human brain. And with that giant noggin comes a complex social life, mysterious communication clicks, and maybe, just maybe, a touch of whale wisdom.

Sperm whales are massive. Adult males can grow up to 16 meters (52 feet) long. They're way too big for most predators to mess with. But young whales and sick adults can sometimes be targeted by orcas (killer whales), who team up in pods to attack. That's why moms are fiercely protective. Even cookie cutter sharks try their luck now and then, chomping out cookie-sized circles of flesh. (Don't worry, the whales usually survive these sharky snacks.)

In the past, humans hunted sperm whales for a special oil called spermaceti, found in their heads. It was used in lamps, machines, and even cosmetics. The hunting was so intense that sperm whale numbers plummeted, pushing them toward extinction. Today, they're listed as vulnerable by the International Union for Conservation of Nature (IUCN), and while their population is slowly recovering, the danger isn't over yet.

Oh. And one last weird but wonderful fact: sperm whales sometimes produce ambergris, a strange, waxy substance formed in their intestines. It's rare, smells unique, and is extremely valuable. Why? Because perfume makers use it to make scents last longer. Yes, some of the world's most expensive perfumes are made with (brace yourself) whale barf.

Deep, strange, and astonishing, the sperm whale reminds us that nature is always full of surprises.

Tripod Fish: Out of the Mud

Imagine trying to live your whole life standing in mud. Not just any mud, but icy, bottom-of-the-ocean, pitch-black mud. That's the challenge faced by the tripod fish, a deep-sea marvel with a clever trick. It never really sits in the mud at all.

The tripod fish, a member of the order *Aulopiformes*, has evolved a rather strange and stylish solution to life in the ooze. It perches on three of its long, stiff fins, one at the tail and two under its belly, like a camera balanced on a tripod. These bony fins stretch up to a meter long, allowing the fish to rise above the soft, squishy seafloor. It's a balancing act worthy of a circus performer, except the audience is mostly sea cucumbers and the occasional wandering shrimp.

But standing still is only part of the tripod fish's survival game. It always faces uphill (yes, there are underwater hills!) so it can catch the flow of water that slides down the slope. This water current carries marine snow, a poetic name for drifting bits of dead plants, animals, and poop that fall

Illustration 63: Tripod fish

from above like a gentle blizzard of leftovers. Mixed into the snow are tiny living creatures, which the tripod fish snaps up with its wide, fang-fringed mouth.

And here's where the story gets even weirder: the tripod fish is a true hermaphrodite. That means every fish is both a boy and a girl at the same time. Talk about versatility! When two tripod fish meet in the darkness of the deep, they can fertilize each other's eggs in a shared exchange of life. But if no one else shows up to the party, which happens a lot in the abyss, the fish can fertilize its own eggs. That's right, the tripod fish is fully self-sufficient, single parent.

Tripod fish spend their entire lives in the Abyssal zone, one of the deepest parts of the ocean, 4,000 meters (over 13,000 feet) below the surface. Down here, it's cold, dark, and incredibly lonely. But the tripod fish is perfectly built for this world of shadows and mud. With its ghostly pale skin, x-ray-like fins, and its patient, upside-down lifestyle, it's one of nature's most unusual and unexpectedly elegant survivors.

So next time you're balancing on one foot or waiting for dinner to arrive, think of the tripod fish: silent, still, and weirdly graceful, standing tall at the very bottom of the sea.

Tube Worms: Methane Munchers of the Deep

Imagine living in a place where poison seeps out of the ground, there's no sunlight, and the pressure could squish a submarine and then thriving there for 250 years. Welcome to the strange and wonderful world of the

Illustration 64: Tube worms

Lamellibrachia luymesi tube worm, a deep-sea champion of survival and teamwork.

Down in the darkest parts of the ocean, where light never reaches and the temperature is chilly, these worms have found a way to turn toxic gas into life-giving food. No, they're not magic (although it sure seems like it). They have a secret helper: bacteria!

These special bacteria live inside a part of the worm's body called the trophosome, which is like a small kitchen tucked into their squishy insides. What's on the menu? Methane. That's right. The same flammable gas used to heat homes can be deadly to us, but for these bacteria, it's a delicious dinner. They "eat" the methane and then share the energy with their tube worm host, like little chefs preparing meals for their clients.

But where do the worms get the methane? They live near cold seeps, which are spooky spots on the ocean floor where methane, oil, and other gooey hydrocarbons leak out of cracks in the Earth's crust. Instead of walking to the grocery store, these tube worms just stick their "feet" (actually a part called a root-like posterior extension) deep into the mud and absorb the methane-rich fluids. Their blood carries the chemicals to the trophosome, and behold, breakfast is served.

These worms grow at a snail's pace, but they can reach an impressive length of three meters (ten feet), about the size of a kayak! Even more amazing, some of them live for 250 years. That means some of the tube worms squirming around down there today might've been alive when Beethoven was composing music.

And tube worms aren't just in it for themselves. As they quietly munch methane and clean the ocean floor of harmful chemicals, they make the neighborhood safer for over a hundred other species such as crabs, shrimp, clams, and even fish. It's like they're running a deep-sea detox spa for ocean creatures.

So next time someone tells you worms are boring, tell them about Lamellibrachia luymesi: the long-lived, deep-diving, methane-cleaning marvels of the sea.

Umbrella Mouth Gulper Eel: Huge Mouth

Illustration 65: Umbrella mouth gulper eel

Imagine a creature with a mouth so enormous, it makes the rest of its body look like an afterthought! Meet the umbrella mouth gulper eel (*Eurypharynx pelecanoides*), one of the oddest, most fascinating fish in the deep sea. Have you ever heard someone say, "Her eyes are bigger than her stomach?" Well, this eel's mouth is bigger than everything! Its jaws can open wide. Really wide. Its stretchy lower jaw forms a giant pouch, just like a pelican's.

But why does this strange eel need such an outsized mouth? Scientists think it's a clever trick for catching dinner. Down in the deep sea, food can be scarce. So if a big swarm of shrimp or other crustaceans drifts by, the gulper eel can simply swim straight into the crowd and gulp down as many as it can in one enormous bite. No nibbling required!

And that's not the eel's only quirk. It has a long, thin, whip-like tail. The tail is so long and delicate, in fact, that gulper eels sometimes get caught with their tails tangled into knots. A knotty fish. What a funny sight that must be!

Now, here's where things get even more magical: the tip of the gulper eel's tail glows. It's dotted with photophores (special light-producing cells) that can shine pink or flash red in the darkness. Scientists think the eel might use this glow as a lure. Since most fish with photophores have them near their mouths (to attract prey close enough to snap up), some researchers wonder if the gulper eel might curl its glowing tail forward, wiggling it like a little neon fishing line to tempt curious shrimp and fish. Since no one has ever seen a gulper eel hunting in the wild, so it remains a tantalizing mystery!

As for swimming, the gulper eel isn't winning any races. With few muscles and that long, floppy body, it moves by gently whipping its tail back and forth. Most likely, it prefers to hang still in the water, blinking its glowing tail, patiently waiting for a meal to wander by.

Gulper eels live in the deep, dark parts of oceans all over the world, usually between 500 and 3,000 meters (about 1,600 to 9,800 feet) below the surface in the mesopelagic zone and bathypelagic zones. It's a cold, shadowy world down there, with very little food and even fewer visitors.

And when it comes to gulper eel romance? That's still a deep-sea mystery, too. Scientists haven't yet observed how they reproduce. The one clue? As male eels grow up, their sense of smell sharpens. Maybe, just maybe, that's how they sniff out a mate in the pitch-black depths.

So the next time you think of the deep sea, picture this remarkable, big-mouthed, light-tipped, knot-tailed eel: an underwater oddball with more mysteries than answers!

Vampire Squid: With a Cloak and Eyes That Glow

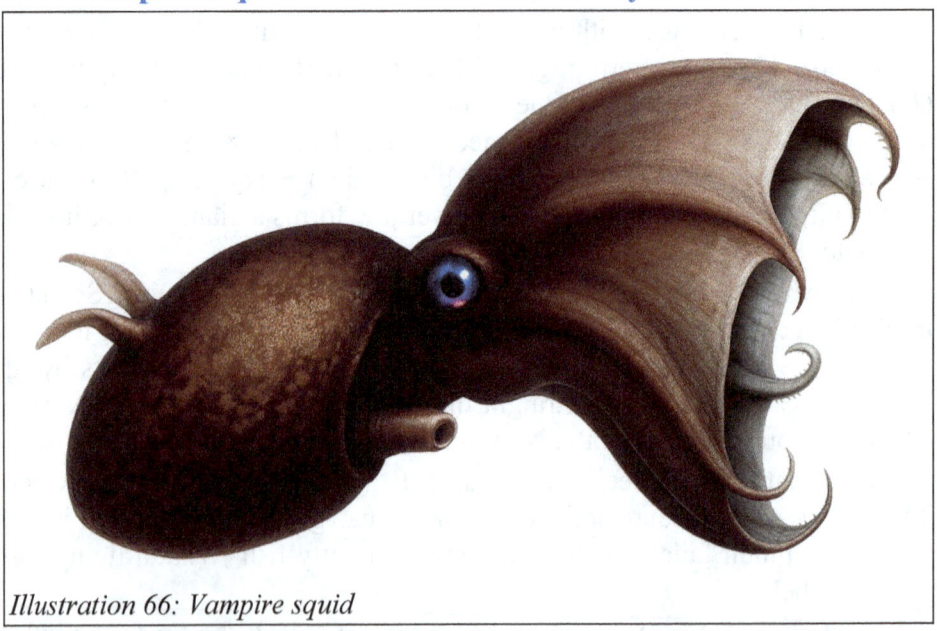

Illustration 66: Vampire squid

Vampyroteuthis infernalis, that's the vampire squid's scientific name. Translated, it means "vampire squid from hell!", a rather dramatic name for a creature that's only about the size of your forearm. But one look at this deep-sea dweller, and you'll see why it earned its spooky title.

The vampire squid's tentacles are connected by a web of dark skin, like a billowing cloak of shadows. Its enormous eyes often glow a haunting red. Drifting silently through the inky depths, it looks like something out of a ghost story. Assuming ghost stories took place a half mile underwater!

The vampire squid lives where the sun's light cannot reach in the mesopelagic and bathypelagic zones: between 600 and 900 meters deep (about 2,000 to 3,000 feet) in a twilight world called the oxygen minimum zone. Down here, there's barely any oxygen and even less food. To survive, the vampire squid runs on low power. It has a super-slow metabolism and blood that's extra good at soaking up oxygen. It's like an ultra-efficient deep-sea vampire, minus the blood-sucking.

Now, you might think a creature named after a vampire would be a fierce hunter. But surprise! The vampire squid is actually more of a scavenger, collecting tiny bits of sinking debris called marine snow. Marine snow is a rain of dead plankton, crustacean shells, and other tasty tidbits that drift down from the surface.

The vampire squid is not defenseless. In fact, the vampire squid is a master of deep-sea illusions! For starters, its skin sparkles with photophores, tiny light-producing organs. This built-in light show is called bioluminescence.

Illustration 67: Vampire squid arms

Of course, glowing in the dark has a downside. It can make you glowing prey. That's why the vampire squid has a clever trick. If startled, it flips its cloak inside out, wrapping its arms around its body. The inner cloak is pitch black, hiding the squid's glowing spots completely. Then, poof! It vanishes into the darkness.

But that's not all! The vampire squid also has counterillumination: it glows gently on its underside to match the faint light filtering from above. To any hungry predator lurking below, the squid becomes invisible, with no shadow to give it away.

And if things get really dicey? The vampire squid can spit glowing mucus! Yep, like a wizard casting a dazzling spell, it ejects a cloud of bluish, glowing goo packed with tiny particles that shine. These lights can twinkle for up to ten minutes which is plenty of time for the vampire squid to make its getaway while the predator is left blinking in confusion.

From hatchling to adult, the vampire squid remains relatively small. It starts life at a tiny 8 millimeters (about ⅓ inch), and grows to about 30 centimeters (1 foot) long. At birth, it carries a yolk sac for nourishment until it can start feeding itself, one more clever adaptation for surviving the deep sea's challenging world.

With giant eyes, glowing skin, a shadowy cloak, and a glittering mucus defense, the vampire squid is one of the ocean's most enchanting and mysterious creatures. It may not be a bloodsucker, but it definitely belongs in the deep-sea hall of fame!

Viperfish: Fish With Fangs

Picture this: long, needle-like fangs flashing through the dark, rushing at you faster than you can blink. If you were a small fish or shrimp, you'd be terrified! Meet the viperfish (genus *Chauliodus*), one of the deep sea's most fearsome hunters.

A viperfish's fangs are so enormous they can't even fit inside its mouth. Instead, when the viperfish closes its jaws, those sharp teeth curve back along its face, right up by its glowing eyes, like a nightmarish smile that never quite goes away.

Illustration 68: Viperfish Chauliodus sloani

But this scary grin isn't just for show. The viperfish has a clever hunting trick. It dangles a tiny glowing lure right in front of its face, staying perfectly still in the dark water. Curious prey swim in close and ZOOM! The viperfish rockets forward, jaws wide, fangs ready. Scientists believe that the viperfish actually spears its prey by ramming into them at high speed, sinking those long teeth deep into their unlucky target.

How does the viperfish survive such a dramatic attack? Its first vertebra is built like a shock absorber, cushioning the force of impact so the fish itself stays safe, while its dinner doesn't stand a chance.

Viperfish enjoy a diet of tasty crustaceans like shrimp and small fish such as anchovies. Thanks to a jaw that hinges open extra wide, they can gulp down prey nearly as big as themselves!

But even a fierce predator has predators of its own. Dragonfish and other larger deep-sea creatures hunt viperfish. To help evade these threats, viperfish have glowing spots called photophores scattered along their body. Scientists think these lights might confuse predators or help the viperfish blend into the faint light above (counterillumination).

An adult viperfish grows between 30 and 60 centimeters long (12 to 24 inches), not too big in a world where everything wants to eat or be eaten. To stay safe, they spend daylight hours in the ocean's twilight zone, between 75 and 1500 meters deep (250 to 5000 feet), int the mesopelagic and bathypelagic zones where sunlight barely reaches. But when night falls, they rise toward shallower waters to hunt where food is more plentiful.

Life in the deep sea is tough, with long stretches between meals. Luckily, viperfish have a very slow metabolism, allowing them to survive for long periods without eating. That's a handy skill when you live where snacks are scarce!

The viperfish family's scientific name is *Chauliodus*, and the best-known species is *Chauliodus sloani*. Because they live so deep and don't survive long in aquariums, scientists still know very little about how viperfish reproduce. The best guess? Females lay eggs that males fertilize them in the open water, but there's still much to discover about these mysterious hunters of the deep.

Zombie Worm: Bone-Eaters of the Deep

What would you name a creature that feasts on the bones of the dead? Scientists call them zombie worms! Their scientific name is *Osedax*, which means "bone devourer", and they certainly live up to it.

Let's imagine. When an animal dies on land, its body doesn't stick around for long. Insects, scavengers, bacteria, and other tiny critters quickly move in for a feast. Bit by bit, the body gets broken down and recycled back into nature. This whole process is called decomposition.

Now, what happens when a giant whale dies in the open ocean? Its body slowly sinks down, down, down, sometimes more than two miles, to the dark, cold seafloor. This is called a whale fall. Down there, an amazing community of deep-sea creatures gathers for an enormous feast. Crabs, hagfish, sea cucumbers, and bacteria all take their share. But, after most of the soft tissues are gone, the bones remain. Bones rich in fats and oils but much harder to crack.

Enter the zombie worms! These tiny worms were first discovered by scientists from the Monterey Bay Aquarium Research Institute. They noticed curious little worms sprouting from whale bones like strange underwater flowers. These were *Osedax mucofloris*, the first zombie worms ever described. Since then, scientists have found more species of zombie worms all over the world's oceans.

Here's where the mystery began: zombie worms don't have mouths, teeth, or even a stomach. So how could they possibly eat something as tough as bone?

Illustration 69: Zombie worm

Scientists soon discovered that zombie worms have an incredible trick. They host special bacteria inside their bodies. These bacteria break down the fats and oils inside the bones and turn them into nutrients the worms can absorb. But how do the worms get inside the bones to reach those nutrients in the first place?

That puzzle stumped scientists for years until researchers at the Scripps Institution of Oceanography solved it. They discovered that zombie worms secrete acid from their skin! This acid slowly dissolves the bone, opening pathways for the worms' root-like structures to burrow inside and reach the nutrient-rich fats. It's like having your very own built-in chemical drill!

Zombie worms are also masters of mystery when it comes to reproduction. When scientists first studied them, they found only female worms. Where were the males? The answer was astonishing. The males were tiny, larval-stage worms living inside the females' bodies! In fact, male zombie worms never grow up. They stay tiny and helpless, their only job being to fertilize the females' eggs. In the world of zombie worms, the girls do all the hunting and the boys stay home forever!

Thanks to these bone-munching wonders, the deep sea recycles every last bit of a whale's body, even the bones. The next time you think of a worm, remember: some of them are dissolving skeletons at the very bottom of the sea!

Learning Activities

Predator/Prey Activity: A Game of Vibrations and Stealth

Can you move like a whisper? Can you listen like a fish? Let's find out!

Big Idea: Using vibrations to detect movement, just like creatures in the wild.

What You'll Need:

A blindfold (or scarf)

A quiet room

At least two daring players (the more, the better!)

What's the Science?

Imagine this: you're a fish deep underwater. You can't see very far, but you can feel tiny ripples of energy moving through the water, vibrations! Those vibrations tell you when something big (or hungry!) is nearby.

Now, let's bring that same idea to air. Vibrations moving through air are called sound waves, and your ears are perfectly designed to catch them. In this game, you'll see how good you are at detecting (or avoiding!) those sneaky sound waves.

How to Play:

Choose Your Roles: One person is the prey. Everyone else will be predators.

Set the Scene: Place the prey in the center of the room. Blindfold them but keep their ears uncovered. The prey needs their super-hearing! Predators start at the edges of the room.

The Hunt Begins: One by one or all at once, for extra fun. Predators will creep silently toward the Prey, trying to get close enough to tap them.

The Prey's Power: The Prey must listen carefully. If they hear a predator, they can point toward where the sound came from. If a predator gets pointed at, they are out! If a predator makes it all the way to the prey and taps them without getting caught, they win! If all Predators are eliminated, the prey claims victory!

Bonus Brainstorm:

After you play, chat about this:
- How did it feel to rely just on sound?
- Were certain types of movement easier to hear?

- How do animals like fish or bats use vibrations or sound to hunt or hide?

Science is everywhere, even in the way you sneak across a room. Now go listen like a fish and stalk like a cat. Good luck!

Water Pressure Activity: Deep Dive

Can you feel the weight of the water? Let's take the plunge and find out!

Big Idea: The deeper you go, the greater the water pressure. Let's see it in action.

What You'll Need:

A swimming pool that's at least 10 feet deep (sorry, bathtubs won't cut it!)

5 empty plastic milk jugs with tight-fitting lids (they work better than soda bottles!)

6 meters (20 feet) of rope

5 kilogram (10 pound) weight (like a dive weight or heavy dumbbell)

String or twine

Swimsuits (because science is splashy sometimes!)

What's the Science?

Water isn't just sitting there, it's pushing on everything it touches. The deeper you go, the more water is stacked above you, and the more it pushes down. This force is called water pressure.

In this experiment, you'll see how milk jugs change shape as they go deeper into the pool. That's water pressure at work!

How to Play (or, How to Be a Water Scientist!):

Prep Your Jugs: Before you dive in, open the lids on your milk jugs to equalize the air pressure inside. Then, screw them on super tight.

Build Your Pressure Chain: Tie the weight to one end of the rope. Now, tie a milk jug right next to the weight. Keep tying the other milk jugs along the rope, one every ½ meter (2 feet) or so. You're creating a vertical chain of jugs.

Time to Dive: Lower (or toss!) the weighted rope into the pool. The weight should sink to the bottom and pull the jugs down at different depths.

Explore & Observe: Swim down alongside the jugs. Look closely. Do they look the same at the bottom as they did near the surface? You might notice some are squished more than others. That's the water pressure increasing with depth!

Record Your Discoveries: After your dive, jot down what you saw:

- Which jug looked the most squished?
- Which one looked unchanged?
- How did the changes match how deep each jug was?

Wonder Time: Why do you think deep-sea creatures look so strange? How do submarines resist all that pressure? What would happen if we used even thinner plastic bottles?

Ready to dive deeper into science? Grab your goggles and go feel the force of the deep!

Density Activity: Sink or Float?

Can you outsmart the water? Let's test the power of density and see what floats your jug!

Big Idea: Objects that are less dense than the fluid around them will float. Objects that are more dense will sink. Sounds simple until you try it!

What You'll Need:

3 plastic milk jugs (empty and clean)

Sand or pebbles

A pool of water (at least 2 feet deep. Deeper is even better!)

What's the Science?

Density is all about how much matter is packed into a space. Think of it this way: a balloon and a rock can be the same size, but one floats and the other sinks because one is full of lighter air and one is full of heavier stuff!

In water, density is a game of gravity and buoyancy:
- If an object is less dense than water → it floats.
- If it's more dense → it sinks.
- If it's just right → it can hover in between!

Fish, submarines, and even giant icebergs use this principle to stay where they want in the water.

How to Play the Density Game:

Prep Your Jugs:
- Jug #1 → fill it with air only. (Put the lid on tight!)
- Jug #2 → fill it all the way to the top with water. (Seal it tight.)
- Jug #3 → fill it with sand or pebbles. (Seal this one too.)

Make Your Prediction:

Before you drop them in, pause for a moment: Which jug do you think will float on top? Which jug will sink to the bottom? Could one jug possibly hover in the middle of the water? Write down your guesses!

Test Time:

Place all three jugs gently into the pool. Watch closely. What happens?

Record Your Results. Which jug floated? Which jug sank? Was any jug surprisingly in between?

Let's Wonder Together:
- Why did each jug behave the way it did?
- What would happen if you filled a jug halfway with water?
- How do fish adjust their density to swim up and down? (Hint: they have something called a swim bladder!)

Next Challenge:

Try using different materials: marbles, foam, coins, oil, etc. Can you create a jug that hovers perfectly in the middle of the pool? That's mastering the art of density!

Water Temperature And Density Activity

Why does deep ocean water stay so cold? Why do icebergs float but icy water sinks? Let's dive into the chilly world of water density!

Big Idea: Water changes density when its temperature changes! Colder water is denser and sinks; warmer water is less dense and floats. That's one reason the deep ocean is always cold. Let's see this in action!

What You'll Need:

2 clear containers (glass bowls or vases work great)

Food coloring

A dropper (or a spoon will do!)

Ice tray

Water

What's the Science?

Water is a shape shifter when it comes to density. At 4°C (just above freezing), water is at its most dense. It sinks to the bottom. As water warms up, it becomes less dense and floats above the colder water. That's why the bottom of the deep ocean hangs out at a chilly 4°C, even though the surface can be much warmer. You'll now create a mini-ocean to watch this temperature-density dance happen before your eyes!

How to Set Up Your Density Dance:

Prep the Ice: Fill an ice tray with water. Add 2 drops of food coloring to each cube. Freeze overnight (or until solid). You've just created cold, colorful "sinking water!"

Prep the Containers: Fill your 2 clear containers with tap water. Let them sit undisturbed for a few hours until they reach room temperature. (Patience here makes the experiment much clearer. Less water movement means better results!)

Time to Experiment:

Step One: The Warm Drop Test

In one container, carefully add 1 drop of food coloring near the surface. Watch what happens. Does it swirl? Sink? Float? How fast does it move? Write down your observations.

Step Two: The Cold Cube Test

In the other container, gently slide one colored ice cube into the water. Watch closely: What happens to the colored melted water as the ice melts? Does it float? Sink? Drift to the bottom? Does it move faster or slower than the warm drop? Record your observations.

Let's Wonder:

Why did the cold water behave differently from the warm drop? Why does deep ocean water stay cold? Does warm water sink to mix with it? How might this affect ocean currents and the movement of nutrients around the planet?

Next-Level Challenge:

Try layering warm water (heat a little water first) on top of room temp water. Can you see the layers? What if you stack cold, warm, and hot water with different colors? (Hint: go slow!)

You've just explored one of the forces that helps shape life on Earth. Oceans are full of invisible rivers of cold and warm water. Now you know why!

Light Absorption Activity

Ever wonder why the deep ocean is so dark? Let's build a mini-ocean and watch the sunlight fade!

Big Idea: The deeper you go in water, the less light makes it through. Each layer of water absorbs some of the light, until eventually, you reach the pitch-black depths. Let's see this in action with our very own tabletop ocean!

What You'll Need:

Several glass drinking glasses (identical shape works best)
Card stock or a roll of heavy paper
Food coloring
A strong flashlight (with fresh batteries, bright light is key!)

Learning Activities

What's the Science?

Sunlight doesn't travel forever in the ocean. As it moves down through the water, each layer absorbs more and more light. That's why the upper layers of the sea are bright, while the deep ocean is cloaked in darkness. In real life, sunlight can only reach about 200 meters into the ocean. Beyond that, it's the realm of shadowy creatures and glowing bioluminescence.

But you don't need an ocean to explore this! We'll create a layered model to watch the light disappear right before our eyes.

How to Build Your Tabletop Ocean:

Fill the Glasses: Fill several glasses with water. Add the same amount of food coloring to each glass.

Build the Light Tunnel: Use your card stock or paper to make a long tunnel that wraps around the glasses in a row. The flashlight will shine through one end, and you'll watch how the light dims as it passes through each "layer." You can even cut little windows between the glasses so you can peek at each stage of light!

Let There Be Light: Turn on your flashlight and aim it down the tunnel through the glasses. Watch carefully. How much light makes it through each glass? What happens to the light by the last glass?

Record Your Discoveries:

Write down your observations: Which glass lets through the most light? Which one seems the darkest? How fast does the light fade?

Let's Wonder:
- Why do you think deep sea animals often glow with their own light?
- How does the color of the water (blue, green, murky) change how far light goes?
- Why do scuba divers lose colors like red and yellow as they go deeper?

Bonus Challenge:

Try using different colors of food coloring. Does red absorb light differently than blue or green? What happens if you use more or fewer glasses? Can you model a shallow sea or a deep trench?

You've just modeled one of the coolest ocean mysteries: Why the deep sea is so dark. Now you know what sunlight faces as it tries to reach the abyss!

Glossary

How to use this glossary:
1) Find the word you want to know more about. The words are listed in alphabetical order.

2) Read the definition. If you don't understand the definition, ask someone to explain it to you.
3) Read the pronunciation. The IPA pronunciation is between the slash marks: /eɪˈfɒ.tɪk/. A IPA pronunciation guide follows this glossary.

absorb /æbˈzɔrb/ to take in; to remove from the environment by taking it into something else.

adapt /ˌædˈæpt/ to make a change that helps an organism survive better in an environment.

algae /ˈæl.dʒi/ a plant with one cell. Plural alga.

ampullae of Lorenzini /ˌæmˈpʊliː əv ˌlɔːrənˈziːni/ tiny, jelly filled pores that can sense electricity in the water.

aphotic /eɪˈfɒ.tɪk/ having little or no light. Parts of the ocean deeper than 200 meters (650 feet) are aphotic.

bacteria /bækˈtər.i.ə/ small, single celled organisms that get their nutrients from the environment.

bioluminescence /baɪ.oʊˌlu.məˈnɛs.əns/ the production of light by living organisms.

biomass /ˈbaɪ oʊˌmæs/ the mass of living things.

black smoker /blæk ˈsmoʊ.kər/ a vent in the ocean floor that spews hot water and chemicals dissolved from magma (hot, liquid rock).

buoyancy /ˈbɔɪənsi/ how something sinks or floats in a liquid.

bud /bʌd/ to produce a bulge that splits apart and becomes a new plant or animal.

camouflage /ˈkæm.əˌflɑʒ/ a way to hide from predators by having colors similar to the environment.

carbon dioxide /ˈkɑr.bən daɪˈɒk.saɪd/ is taken in by plants and oxygen is returned to the environment. Oxygen is taken in by animals and carbon dioxide is returned to the environment.

carnivore /ˈkɑr.nəˌvoʊr/ an animal that eats other animals.

cartilage /ˈkɑrt.lɪdʒ/ a flexible tissue that supports body and muscles.

cell /sɛl/ a walled blob of living matter with DNA and other structures that help it keep alive.

Celsius /ˈsɛl.si.əs/ the most commonly used temperature scale. At sea level, water freezes at about 0° Celsius and boils at 100° Celsius.

cephalopod /ˈsɛf.ə.ləˌpɒd/ sea creatures that have tentacles around their mouths, such as squid and octopuses.

chemosynthesis /ˌkiːmoʊˈsɪnθəsɪs/ a process where certain bacteria make their own food using energy from chemicals such as hydrogen sulfide, and do not use sunlight.

chromatophore /krəˈmæt.əˌfɔr/ a cell containing colored pigments that opens and closes to change color.

cold-blooded /koʊld ˈblʌd.ɪd/ body temperature is the same as the environment around it.
colony /ˈkɒl.ə.ni/ a group of animals that live and work together.
continental shelf /ˌkɒn.tnˈɛn.tl ʃɛlf/ part of a continent, formed from eroded soil washed to the ocean, which is relatively shallow.
continental slope /ˌkɒn.tnˈɛn.tl sloʊp/ a steep slope that goes from the continental shelf to the deep ocean.
conserve /kənˈsɜːrv/ protected, saved, or kept from being used up or lost.
copepod /ˈkoʊ.pəˌpɒd/ a small crustacean that can drift at sea or live on the bottom of the ocean.
counterillumination /ˈkaʊn.tər ɪˌlu.məˈneɪ ʃən/ having bioluminescence on the underside to mimic the glow of light from the surface.
crustacean /krʌˈsteɪ.ʃən/ a class of animals that often live in water and have a hard shell, such as lobsters, crayfish, crabs and shrimp.
decomposition /ˌdi.kɒm.pəˈzɪ.ʃən/ the breaking down of dead tissue, usually by bacteria.
density /ˈdɛn.sɪ.ti/ how much matter is contained in a given volume.
depth /dɛpθ/ how far below a surface.
digest /dɪˈdʒɛst/ to break down food so that it can be absorbed by the body.
DNA /ˈdi ɛn eɪ/ Deoxyribonucleic acid, a molecule which can be copied easily, and which determines how living organisms form.
egg /ɛg/ a reproductive unit containing an embryo and food for the embryo.
embryo /ˈɛm.briˌoʊ/ an animal in the early stages of development, usually in an egg or in a mother's womb.
energy /ˈɛn.ər.dʒi/ any source of usable power, such as solar energy or chemical energy.
environment /ɛnˈvaɪ.ərn.mənt/ everything that is around a plant or animal.
epipelagic /ˌɛp.i.pəˈlædʒ.ɪk/ the layer of open ocean from the surface to 200 meters (650 feet) deep.
essential /əˈsɛn.ʃəl/ necessary; something that must exist or happen.
exoskeleton /ˌɛk.soʊˈskɛl.ɪ.tn/ a hard shell that covers the outside of some animals, such as crustaceans.
extinct /ɪkˈstɪŋkt/ the species is absent from Earth.
Fahrenheit /ˈfær.ənˌhaɪt/ a temperature scale where water freezes at 32° and boils at 212°.
feces /ˈfi.siz/ poop; what is left over after an animal finishes digesting its food.
fecal /ˈfiː.kəl/ having to do with poop.
female /ˈfi.meɪl/ a girl; produces eggs.
fertilize /ˈfɜr.tlˌaɪz/ to combine sperm and eggs so that the eggs become a living creature.

filter feeder /ˈfɪl.tər ˈfi.dər/ an animal that eats by collecting tiny plants and animals from the water.

fluorescence /fluˈrɛsəns/ one color of light is absorbed, and a different color in emitted.

fossil /ˈfɒs.əl/ a rock that shows the shape of something that lived long ago.

gastrozooid /ˌgæs.troʊˈzoʊ.ɔɪd/ an animal that is part of a colony that feeds for the colony.

gelatinous /ˈdʒɛl.ɑ.tn.ʌs/ having a consistency like jelly.

giantism /ˈdʒaɪ.ənˌtɪz.əm/ the fact that many deep sea creatures grow much larger than similar creatures in the shallow part of the ocean.

gill /gɪl/ an organ that lets a fish breath under water by pulling oxygen from the water.

gill raker /gɪl ˈreɪ.kər/ an organ like a comb in a filter feeder's mouth that guides plankton into the fishes stomach.

habitat-forming /ˈhæb.ɪˌtæt ˈfɔrm.ɪŋ/ makes a place for other creatures to live.

hemoglobin /ˈhiːməˌgloʊbɪn/ a molecule in blood that carries oxygen.

hermaphrodite /hɜrˈmæf.rəˌdaɪt/ an animal that produces both eggs and sperm.

herbivore /ˈhɜr.bəˌvoʊr/ an animal that eats plants.

host /hoʊst/
1) an animal or plant that is infected with a parasite.
2) an animal or plant or environment that creates an inviting area for other to live in.

hunt /hʌnt/ to search for and catch animals to eat.

hydrothermal vent /ˌhaɪdroʊˈθɜːrməl vɛnt/ see thermal vent page 95.

invertebrate /ɪnˈvɜːrtɪbrət/ does not have vertebrae protecting a spinal cord.

larva /ˈlɑr.və/ the form of an animal when it is young. Larvae often look different from the adults. Plural: larvae.

lateral line /ˈlæt.ər.əl laɪn/ a set of cells along the side of a fish's body that sense vibration in the water.

life /laɪf/ all things that gets energy from a source and uses it to make body tissue.

liquid /ˈlɪk.wɪd/ any substance that can flow like water.

living fossil /ˈlɪv.ɪŋ ˈfɒs.əl/ A plant or animal that lived long ago with little change.

magma /ˈmæg.mə/ molten rock from the earth's core.

male /meɪl/ a boy; produces sperm.

marine snow /məˈrin snoʊ/ pieces of dead plants and animals, and feces of animals that drift down from upper layers.

mass /mæs/
1) The amount of matter in an object.
2) A usually shapeless object that that is all one piece.

mate /meɪt/
1) to combine sperm and eggs.
2) another creature of the opposite sex with which sperm and eggs will be combined.

mesopelagic /ˌmɛz.ə.pəˈlædʒ.ɪk/ open ocean at a depth between 180 meters (600 feet) and 900 meters (3,000 feet).

metabolism /məˈtæb.əˌlɪz.əm/ how fast an animal uses energy.

microscopic /ˌmaɪkrəˈskɑːpɪk/ so small that a person must use a microscope to see it.

migrate /ˈmaɪ.greɪt/ to move from one region to another on a regular basis.

molt /moʊlt/ to shed a skin or exoskeleton all at once, uncovering a new skin or skeleton that has already grown underneath.

nectophore /nɛk.taʊˈfaʊɚ/ a zooid that specializes in swimming.

nectosome /nɛk.taʊˈzaʊm/ a group of zooids that specialize in swimming, usually at the center of a siphonophore.

nutrient /ˈnu.tri.ənt/ something that is used for food.

ocean floor /ˈoʊ.ʃən flour/ a flat part of the bottom of the ocean.

omnivore /ˈɒm.nəˌvoʊr/ an animal that eats both plants and animals.

organ /ˈɔr.gən/ a group of cells that work together for a purpose.

organic /ɔrˈgæn.ɪk/ contains carbon

organism /ˈɔr.gəˌnɪz.əm/ a living thing.

overfishing /ˈoʊ.vərˈfɪʃ.ɪŋ/ fishing so much that fish can not recover easily.

oxygen /ˈɒk.sɪ.dʒən/ an element that combines with carbon to make carbon dioxide.

photic /ˈfoʊ.tɪk/ having light. The top 200 meters (650 feet) of the ocean is photic.

photophore /ˈfoʊ.təˌfor/ a light producing organ.

photosynthesis /ˌfoʊtoʊˈsɪnθəsɪs/ The process where plants, algae, and some bacteria use sunlight to make their own food.

pigment /ˈpɪg.mənt/ a chemical that has a particular color.

plankton /ˈplæŋk.tən/ a small plant or animal that lives in the ocean and drifts with the ocean currents.

pneumatophore /ˈnuː.mə.təˌfɔɹ/ a zooid that helps a colony float up and down.

predator /ˈprɛd əˌtɔr/ an animal that hunts and eats other animals.

pressure /ˈprɛʃ.ər/ force pressing against the surface of an object.

prey /preɪ/ an animal that is hunted for food.

reproduction /ˌri.prəˈdʌk.ʃən/
  1) how babies are made.
  2) the process of making babies.
scale /skeɪl/ a thin, hard plate that covers the skin of most fish.
scarce /skɛrs/ enough of it to go around, in short supply, hard to find.
scarcity /ˈskɛrsəti/ that state of being scarce.
scavenge /ˈskæv.ɪndʒ/ to search around for dead animals to eat.
scavenger /ˈskæv.ɪn.dʒər/ an animal that eats dead animals.
secrete /sɪˈkrit/ to make and release, usually from a gland. Example: The Atlantic hagfish secretes a sticky slime.
sexual dimorphism /ˈsɛk.ʃu.əl daɪˈmɔr.fɪz.əm/ males and females look very different.
shell /ʃɛl/
  1) a hard covering inside of which an animal lives.
  2) an exoskeleton.
sperm /spɜrm/ a cell produced by a male that contains half of the genetic material to make a baby.
stage /steɪdʒ/ a time period in the development of an animal, often accompanied by changes in form.
surface /ˈsɜr.fɪs/ where the ocean meets the air in the atmosphere.
survive /sərˈvaɪv/ to continue to live. To not die.
swim /swɪm/ to move through water under one's own power.
swim bladder /swɪm ˈblæd.ər/ a sac that can be filled and emptied of air to make a fish sink towards the bottom, or rise towards the top.
symbiosis /ˌsɪm.baɪˈoʊ.sɪs/ a mutually beneficial relationship between two different creatures.
temperature /ˈtɛm.pər.ə.tʃər/ how hot or how cold.
tentacle /ˈtɛn.tə.kəl/ a thin, flexible arm without bones that has muscles to allow it to move. *Example*: An octopus has eight tentacles.
thermal vent /ˈθɜr.məl vɛnt/ a crack in the earth's crust at the bottom of the ocean where magma is near the surface. Also called a hydrothermal vent.
thermocline /ˈθɜr.məˌklaɪn/ ocean water gradually changes temperature with depth.
threatened /ˈθrɛt.nd/ placed in danger.
tissue /ˈtɪʃ.u/ a mass of cells forming a structure, such as skin tissue.
translucent /trænzˈlu.sənt/ some light can go through it. Partially see-through.
twilight /ˈtwaɪˌlaɪt/ the part of the day after the sun has gone down, but before all the sunlight has gone from the sky.
vertebra /ˈvɜr.tə.brə/ a backbone which holds the spinal cord. Plural: vertebrae.

vertical migration /ˈvɜr.tɪ.kəl maɪˈgreɪ.ʃən/ Moving up and down in the water column on a regular basis.
vibration /vaɪˈbreɪ.ʃən/ a wave like a sound wave that moves through water. Vibrations are caused by something moving in the water.
worm /wɜrm/ a long, thin animal that usually lives on the ocean floor.
yolk /youlk/ the part of the egg that provides food for the fetus.
zooid /ˈzoʊ.ɔɪd/ an individual animal that is part of a larger colonial animal.
zooplankton /ˌzoʊˈplæŋk.tən/ small animals that drift with the currents.

IPA Pronunciation

Stress marks: /ˈ/ primary; /ˌ/ secondary

Consonants

b	<u>b</u>ase, dou<u>b</u>le
d	<u>d</u>isk, an<u>d</u>
ð	<u>th</u>e, fa<u>th</u>er
dʒ	<u>g</u>eneral, <u>p</u>age
f	<u>f</u>rom, gra<u>ph</u>, <u>f</u>an
g	<u>g</u>et, an<u>g</u>le
h	<u>h</u>ead, a<u>h</u>ead
j	<u>y</u>es
k	<u>ch</u>ord, fa<u>c</u>t, <u>k</u>ey
l	<u>l</u>ow, s<u>l</u>ow
m	<u>m</u>iddle, ti<u>m</u>e
n	<u>n</u>ot, i<u>n</u>
ŋ	thi<u>ng</u>, lo<u>ng</u>
ŋg	fi<u>ng</u>er, a<u>ng</u>le
θ	<u>th</u>ird, ma<u>th</u>
p	<u>p</u>i, ca<u>p</u>
ɹ	<u>r</u>ow, f<u>r</u>om
s	<u>s</u>ide, ba<u>s</u>e
ʃ	~~sh~~ow, addi<u>ti</u>on
t	<u>t</u>rue, wri<u>t</u>e
tʃ	<u>ch</u>eck, ca<u>tch</u>
v	<u>v</u>alue, ha<u>v</u>e
w	<u>w</u>ave, s<u>w</u>ap
ʰw	<u>wh</u>y
z	<u>z</u>ero, i<u>s</u>
ʒ	mea<u>s</u>ure, divi<u>si</u>on

Vowels

ɑ	f<u>a</u>ther
ɑɹ	<u>ar</u>c, b<u>ar</u>n
ɒ	s<u>o</u>ng, s<u>o</u>lid
ɒɹ	b<u>o</u>rrow
æ	<u>a</u>dd, <u>a</u>ngle
æɹ	<u>arr</u>ow, m<u>arr</u>y
aɪ	b<u>y</u>, s<u>i</u>gn
aʊ	<u>ou</u>t, h<u>ow</u>
aʊɚ	h<u>our</u>
ɛ	b<u>e</u>ll
ɛɹ	<u>err</u>or
ɛɚ	sq<u>uare</u>, <u>are</u>a
eɪ	f<u>a</u>ce, r<u>a</u>te
ɪ	<u>i</u>n, l<u>i</u>d
ɪɹ	g<u>ir</u>l
ɪɚ	n<u>ear</u>, z<u>ero</u>
ɔɪ	ch<u>oi</u>ce, b<u>oy</u>, p<u>oi</u>nt
ɔɹ	ch<u>or</u>d, c<u>or</u>ner
oʊ	r<u>ow</u>, g<u>o</u>
ʊ	f<u>oo</u>t
ʌ	<u>o</u>f, n<u>u</u>mber
ɝ	c<u>ur</u>ve, c<u>ir</u>cle
u	contin<u>ue</u>
y	c<u>u</u>be

Reduced vowels

ə	comm<u>a</u>
ɚ	cent<u>er</u>
i	happ<u>y</u>
o	g<u>o</u>ld

Image Credits

All images not listed here are copyright 2025 David E. McAdams. All rights reserved.

Bluntnose sixgill shark lower jaw, D Ross Robertson, Smithsonian Institution, Public domain.

Cold deep corals in the Bay of Biscay, title page, Licensed under the Creative Commons Attribution 4.0 International license. https://image.ifremer.fr/data/00534/64548/.

Deep sea coral, page 41, NOAA, Public domain.

Giant isopod, page 50, Kentaro Ohno さん, This file is licensed under the Creative Commons Attribution 2.0 Generic license.

Giant tube worm, page 52, NOAA, Public domain.

Gummy squirrel, page 55, NOAA. Public domain.

Helmet jellyfish, page 56, NOAA. Public domain.

Japanese spider crab, page 57, Lukas Reimann, This file is made available under the Creative Commons CC0 1.0 Universal Public domain Dedication.

Oceans of the World, page 15, Nowakowska, Joanna; Sobocińska, Joanna; Lewicki, Mateusz; Lemańska, Żaneta; Rzymski, Piotr (2020). Image modified to show oceans of the world. Licensed under the Creative Commons Attribution 4.0 International license. https://commons.wikimedia.org/wiki/File:When_science_goes_viral_-_The_research_response_during_three_months_of_the_COVID-19_outbreak_-_Fig._4.jpg

Parts of a fish, George Chernilevsky, page 20, Public domain, image modified to label the parts of a fish.

Siphonophore, page 72, Catriona Munro, Stefan Siebert, Felipe Zapata, Mark Howison, Alejandro Damian-Serrano, Samuel H. Church, Freya E.Goetz, Philip R. Pugh, Steven H.D.Haddock, Casey W.Dun, this file is licensed under the Creative Commons Attribution 4.0 International license. Image modified to remove key letters.

Tripod fish, page 76, NOAA Okeanos Explorer Program, Public domain.

www.ingramcontent.com/pod-product-compliance
Lightning Source LLC
Chambersburg PA
CBHW070122080526
44586CB00013B/1356